D0907107

Reason in Human Affairs

The Harry Camp Lectures at
Stanford University, 1982

The Harry Camp Memorial Fund
was established in 1959 to make
possible a continuing series of
lectures at Stanford University on
topics bearing on the dignity and
worth of the human individual.

HERBERT A. SIMON

Reason in Human Affairs

STANFORD UNIVERSITY PRESS   1983
STANFORD, CALIFORNIA

Stanford University Press
Stanford, California
© 1983 by the Board of Trustees of the
Leland Stanford Junior University
Printed in the United States of America
ISBN 0-8047-1179-8
LC 82-62448

To the Memory of
JASCHA MARSCHAK
who had an unshakeable faith in
human reason, and an unmatched
store of human warmth

Preface

THE NATURE of human reason—its mechanisms, its effects, and its consequences for the human condition—has been my central preoccupation for nearly fifty years. When the invitation came to deliver the Harry Camp Lectures at Stanford University, I wondered if I had anything left to say on the subject. And if there were some such topic, had it not already been thoroughly investigated by such friends on the Stanford campus as Kenneth Arrow, James March, and Amos Tversky—to mention just a few who work in one part or another of this domain? Putting aside this concern, real though it is, I decided to use the occasion of the lectures to explore some byways that seemed to me interesting and important, but that had until now been off the main paths of my own explorations.

Three topics, especially, were the objects of my inquiry: the relation of reason to intuition and emotion, the analogy between rational adaptation and evolution, and the implications of bounded rationality for the operation of social and political institutions. In the chapters that follow, I report on these topics within the framework provided by the general viewpoint of bounded rationality.

I am indebted to Stanford University for the occasion

and opportunity to prepare these pages, and for the hospitality and stimulation I always enjoy on my visits to the Stanford campus. I am grateful, too, to Donald T. Campbell, Richard C. Lewontin, and Edward O. Wilson, who provided valuable criticisms of a draft of Chapter 2, though it is not to be assumed that they would agree with everything in the final version of that chapter. To them, and to many friends who have helped guide my education on evolutionary theory and on other topics addressed in these pages, I offer my warm thanks.

H.A.S.

Contents

Reason in Human Affairs

are capable of generating normative outputs purely from descriptive inputs.[1] The corollary to "no conclusions without premises" is "no *ought*'s from *is*'s alone." Thus, whereas reason may provide powerful help in finding means to reach our ends, it has little to say about the ends themselves.

There is a final difficulty, first pointed out by Gödel, that rich systems of logic are never complete—there always exist true theorems that cannot be reached as outputs by applying the legal transformations to the inputs. Since the problem of logical incompleteness is much less important in the application of reason to human affairs than the difficulties that concern us here, I shall not discuss it further. Nor will I be concerned with whether the standard axioms of logic and the rules of inference themselves are to some extent arbitrary. For the purpose of this discussion, I shall regard them as unexceptionable.

Reason, then, goes to work only after it has been supplied with a suitable set of inputs, or premises. If reason is to be applied to discovering and choosing courses of action, then those inputs include, at the least, a set of *should*'s, or values to be achieved, and a set of *is*'s, or facts about the world in which the action is to be taken. Any attempt to justify these *should*'s and *is*'s by logic will simply lead to a regress to new *should*'s and *is*'s that are similarly postulated.

VALUES

We see that reason is wholly instrumental. It cannot tell us where to go; at best it can tell us how to get there. It is a

---

[1] I will not undertake to make the argument here. It was stated well many years ago by Ayer, in *Language, Truth, and Logic*, rev. ed. (New York, 1946), chap. 6.

gun for hire that can be employed in the service of whatever goals we have, good or bad. It makes a great difference in our view of the human condition whether we attribute our difficulties to evil or to ignorance and irrationality—to the baseness of goals or to our not knowing how to reach them.

Method in Madness

A useful, if outrageous, exercise for sharpening one's thinking about the limited usefulness of reasoning, taken in isolation, is to attempt to read Hitler's *Mein Kampf* analytically—as though preparing for a debate. The exercise is likely to be painful, but is revealing about how facts, values, and emotions interact in our thinking about human affairs. I pick this particular example because the reader's critical faculties are unlikely, in this case, to be dulled by agreement with the views expressed.

Most of us would take exception to many of Hitler's "facts," especially his analysis of the causes of Europe's economic difficulties, and most of all his allegations that Jews and Marxists (whom he also mistakenly found indistinguishable) were at the root of them. However, if we were to suspend disbelief for a moment and accept his "facts" as true, much of the Nazi program would be quite consistent with goals of security for the German nation or even of welfare for the German people. Up to this point, the unacceptability of that program to us is not a matter of evil goals—no one would object to concern for the welfare of the German people—or of faulty reasoning from those goals, but rests on the unacceptability of the factual postulates that connect the goals to the program. From this viewpoint, we might decide that the remedy for Nazism was to combat its program by reason resting on better factual premises.

But somehow that calm response does not seem to match the outrage that *Mein Kampf* produces in us. There must be something more to our rejection of its argument, and obviously there is. Its stated goals are, to put it mildly, incomplete. Statements of human goals usually distinguish between a "we" for whom the goals are shaped and a "they" whose welfare is not "our" primary concern. Hitler's "we" was the German people—the definition of "we" being again based on some dubious "facts" about a genetic difference between Aryan and non-Aryan peoples. Leaving aside this fantasy of Nordic purity, most of us would still define "we" differently from Hitler. Our "we" might be Americans instead of Germans, or, if we had reached a twenty-first-century state of enlightenment, our "we" might even be the human species. In either case, we would be involved in a genuine value conflict with *Mein Kampf*, a conflict not resolvable in any obvious way by improvements in either facts or reasoning. Our postulation of a "we"—of the boundary of our concern for others—is a basic assumption about what is good and what is evil.

Probably the greatest sense of outrage that *Mein Kampf* generates stems from the sharpness of the boundary Hitler draws between "we" and "they." Not only does he give priority to "we," but he argues that any treatment of "they," however violent, is justifiable if it advances the goals of "we." Even if Hitler's general goals and "facts" were accepted, most of us would still object to the measures he proposes to inflict on "they" in order to nurture the welfare of "we." If, in our system of values, we do not regard "they" as being without rights, reason will disclose to us a conflict of values—a conflict between our value of helping "we" and our general goal of not inflicting harm on "they." And so it is not its reasoning for which we must fault *Mein Kampf*, but its alleged facts and its outrageous values.

There is another lesson to be learned from *Mein Kampf*. We cannot read many lines of it before detecting that Hitler's reasoning is not cold reasoning but hot reasoning. We have long since learned that when a position is declaimed with passion and invective, there is special need to examine carefully both its premises and its inferences. We have learned this, but we do not always practice it. Regrettably, it is precisely when the passion and invective resonate with our own inner feelings that we forget the warning and become uncritical readers or listeners.

Hitler was an effective rhetorician for Germans precisely because his passion and invectives resonated with beliefs and values already present in many German hearts. The heat of his rhetoric rendered his readers incapable of applying the rules of reason and evidence to his arguments. Nor was it only Germans who resonated to the facts and values he proclaimed. The latent anti-Semitism and overt anti-Communism of many Western statesmen made a number of his arguments plausible to them.

And so we learned, by bitter experience and against our first quick judgments, that we could not dismiss Hitler as a madman, for there was method in his madness. His prose met standards of reason neither higher nor lower than we are accustomed to encountering in writing designed to persuade. Reason was not, could not have been, our principal shield against Nazism. Our principal shield was contrary factual beliefs and values.

De Gustibus Est Disputandum

Recognizing all these complications in the use of reason, hot or cold, and recognizing also that *ought*'s cannot be derived from *is*'s alone, we must still admit that it is possible to reason about conduct. For most of the *ought*'s we profess are not ultimate standards of conduct but only subgoals, adopted as means to other goals. For example, taken in isolation a goal like "live within your income" may sound unassailable. Yet a student might be well advised to go into debt in order to complete his or her education. A debt incurred as an investment in future productivity is different from a gambling debt.

Values can indeed be disputed (1) if satisfying them has consequences, present or future, for other values, (2) if they are acquired values, or (3) if they are instrumental to more final values. But although there has been widespread consensus about the rules of reasoning that apply to factual matters, it has proved far more difficult over the centuries to reach agreement about the rules that should govern reasoning about interrelated values. Several varieties of modal logic proposed for reasoning about imperative and deontic statements have gained little acceptance and even less application outside of philosophy.[2]

In the past half century, however, an impressive body of formal theory has been erected by mathematical statisti-

---

[2]I state the case against modal logics in Section 3 of my *Models of Discovery* (Dordrecht, 1977) and in "On Reasoning about Actions," chap. 8 of H. A. Simon and L. Siklóssy, eds., *Representation and Meaning* (Englewood Cliffs, N.J., 1972).

cians and economists to help us reason about these matters—without introducing a new kind of logic. The basic idea of this theory is to load all values into a single function, the utility function, in this way finessing the question of how different values are to be compared. The comparison has in effect already been made when it is assumed that a utility has been assigned to each particular state of affairs.

This formal theory is called subjective expected utility (SEU) theory. Its construction is one of the impressive intellectual achievements of the first half of the twentieth century. It is an elegant machine for applying reason to problems of choice. Our next task is to examine it, and to make some judgments about its validity and limitations.

SUBJECTIVE EXPECTED UTILITY

Since a number of comprehensive and rigorous accounts of SEU theory are available in the literature,[3] I will give here only a brief heuristic survey of its main components.

The Theory

First, the theory assumes that a decision maker has a well-defined *utility function*, and hence that he can assign a cardinal number as a measure of his liking of any particular scenario of events over the future. Second, it assumes that the decision maker is confronted with a well-defined *set of alternatives* to choose from. These alternatives need not be one-time choices, but may involve sequences of choices or strategies in which each subchoice will be made only at a specified time using the information available at that time.

---

[3] For example, L. J. Savage's classic, *The Foundations of Statistics* (New York, 1954).

Third, it assumes that the decision maker can assign a consistent *joint probability distribution* to all future sets of events. Finally, it assumes that the decision maker will (or should) choose the alternative, or the strategy, that will *maximize the expected value*, in terms of his utility function, of the set of events consequent on the strategy. With each strategy, then, is associated a probability distribution of future scenarios that can be used to weight the utilities of those scenarios.

These are the four principal components of the SEU model: a cardinal utility function, an exhaustive set of alternative strategies, a probability distribution of scenarios for the future associated with each strategy, and a policy of maximizing expected utility.

Problems with the Theory

Conceptually, the SEU model is a beautiful object deserving a prominent place in Plato's heaven of ideas. But vast difficulties make it impossible to employ it in any literal way in making actual human decisions. I have said so much about these difficulties at other times and places (particularly in the pages of *Administrative Behavior*) that I will make only the briefest mention of them here.

The SEU model assumes that the decision maker contemplates, in one comprehensive view, everything that lies before him. He understands the range of alternative choices open to him, not only at the moment but over the whole panorama of the future. He understands the consequences of each of the available choice strategies, at least up to the point of being able to assign a joint probability distribution to future states of the world. He has reconciled or balanced all his conflicting partial values and synthesized them into a single utility function that orders, by his preference for them, all these future states of the world.

The SEU model finesses completely the origins of the values that enter into the utility function; they are simply there, already organized to express consistent preferences among all alternative futures that may be presented for choice. The SEU model finesses just as completely the processes for ascertaining the facts of the present and future states of the world. At best, the model tells us how to reason about fact and value premises; it says nothing about where they come from.

When these assumptions are stated explicitly, it becomes obvious that SEU theory has never been applied, and never can be applied—with or without the largest computers—in the real world. Yet one encounters many purported applications in mathematical economics, statistics, and management science. Examined more closely, these applications retain the formal structure of SEU theory, but substitute for the incredible decision problem postulated in that theory either a highly abstracted problem in a world simplified to a few equations and variables, with the utility function and the joint probability distributions of events assumed to be already provided, or a microproblem referring to some tiny, carefully defined and bounded situation carved out of a larger real-world reality.

SEU as an Approximation

Since I have had occasion to use SEU theory in some of my own research in management science, let me throw the stone through my own window. Holt, Modigliani, Muth, and I constructed a procedure for making decisions about production levels, inventories, and work force in a factory under conditions of uncertainty.[4] The procedure fits the SEU model. The utility function is (the negative of) a cost function, comprising costs of production, costs of changing the level of production, putative costs of lost orders, and inventory holding costs. The utility function is assumed to be quadratic in the independent variables, an assumption made because it is absolutely essential if the mathematics and computation are to be manageable. Expected values for sales in each future period are assumed to be known. (The same assumption of the quadratic utility function fortunately makes knowledge of the complete probability distributions irrelevant.) The factory is assumed to have a single homogeneous product, or a set of products that can legitimately be represented by a single-dimensional aggregate.

It is clear that if this decision procedure is used to make decisions for a factory, that is very different from employing SEU theory to make decisions in the real world. All but one of the hard questions have been answered in advance by the assumption of a known, quadratic criterion function and known expected values of future sales. Moreover, this single set of production decisions has been carved out of the entire array of decisions that management has to make, and it has been assumed to be describable in a fashion that is completely independent of information about those other decisions or about any other aspect of the real world.

I have no urge to apologize for our decision procedure

---

[4]C. C. Holt, F. Modigliani, J. R. Muth, and H. A. Simon, *Planning Production, Inventories and Work Force* (Englewood Cliffs, N.J., 1960).

as a useful management science tool. It can be, and has been, applied to this practical decision task in a number of factory situations and seems to have operated satisfactorily. What I wish to emphasize is that it is applied to a highly simplified representation of a tiny fragment of the real-world situation, and that the goodness of the decisions it will produce depends much more on the adequacy of the approximating assumptions and the data supporting them than it does on the computation of a maximizing value according to the prescribed SEU decision rule. Hence, it would be perfectly conceivable for someone to contrive a quite different decision procedure, outside the framework of SEU theory, that would produce better decisions in these situations (measured by real-world consequences) than would be produced by our decision rule.

Exactly the same comments can be made about economic models formed within the SEU mold. Their veridicality and usefulness cannot be judged from the fact that they satisfy, formally, the SEU assumptions. In evaluating them, it is critical to know how close the postulated utilities and future events match those of the real world.

Once we accept the fact that, in any actual application, the SEU rule supplies only a crude approximation to an abstraction, an outcome that may or may not provide satisfactory solutions to the real-world problems, then we are free to ask what other decision procedures, unrelated to SEU, might also provide satisfactory outcomes. In particular, we are free to ask what procedures human beings actually use in their decision making and what relation those actual procedures bear to the SEU theory.

I hope I have persuaded you that, in typical real-world

situations, decision makers, no matter how badly they want to do so, simply cannot apply the SEU model. If doubt still remains on this point, it can be dissipated by examining the results of laboratory experiments in which human subjects have been asked to make decisions involving risk and uncertainty in game-like situations orders of magnitude simpler than the game of real life. The evidence, much of which has been assembled in several articles by Amos Tversky and his colleagues, leaves no doubt whatever that the human behavior in these choice situations—for whatever reasons—departs widely from the prescriptions of SEU theory.[5] Of course, I have already suggested what the principal reason is for this departure. It is that human beings have neither the facts nor the consistent structure of values nor the reasoning power at their disposal that would be required, even in these relatively simple situations, to apply SEU principles.

As our next task, we consider what they do instead.

THE BEHAVIORAL ALTERNATIVE

I will ask you to introspect a bit about how you actually make decisions, and I will make some assertions that you can check against your introspections. First, your decisions are not comprehensive choices over large areas of your life, but are generally concerned with rather specific matters, assumed, whether correctly or not, to be relatively independent of other, perhaps equally important, dimensions of life. At the moment you are buying a car, you are probably not also simultaneously choosing next

[5] See A. Tversky and D. Kahnemann, "Judgment under Uncertainty: Heuristics and Biases," *Science* 185: 1124–31 (1974), and references cited there.

week's dinner menu, or even deciding how to invest income you plan to save.

Second, when you make any particular decision, even an important one, you probably do not work out detailed scenarios of the future, complete with probability distributions, conditional on the alternative you choose. You have a general picture of your life-style and prospects, and perhaps of one or two major contemplated changes in the near future, and even of a couple of contingencies. When you are considering buying a car, you have a general notion of your use of automobiles, your income and the other demands on it, and whether you are thinking of getting a new job in another city. You are unlikely to envision large numbers of other possibilities that might affect what kind of car it makes sense to buy.

Third, the very fact that you are thinking about buying a car, and not a house, will probably focus your attention on some aspects of your life and some of your values to the relative neglect of others. The mere contemplation of buying a car may stimulate fond memories or dreams of travel, and divert your attention from the pleasures of listening to stereo or giving dinner parties for friends at home. Hence, it is unlikely that a single comprehensive utility function will watch over the whole range of decisions you make. On the contrary, particular decision domains will evoke particular values, and great inconsistencies in choice may result from fluctuating attention. We all know that if we want to diet, we should resist exposing ourselves to tempting food. That would be neither necessary nor useful if our choices were actually guided by a single comprehensive and consistent utility function.

Fourth, a large part of whatever effort you devote to making your car-buying decision will be absorbed in gathering facts and evoking possibly relevant values. You may read *Consumer Reports* and consult friends; you may visit car dealers in order to learn more about the various alternatives, and to learn more about your own tastes as well. Once facts of this sort have been assembled, and preferences evoked, the actual choice may take very little time.

Bounded Rationality

Choices made in the general way I have just been describing are sometimes characterized as instances of *bounded rationality*. Good reasons can be given for supposing that evolutionary processes might produce creatures capable of bounded rationality. Moreover, a great deal of psychological research supports the hunch to which our introspections have led us, namely that this is the way in which human decisions—even the most deliberate—are made. Let us call this model of human choice the behavioral model, to contrast it with the Olympian model of SEU theory.

Within the behavioral model of bounded rationality, one doesn't have to make choices that are infinitely deep in time, that encompass the whole range of human values, and in which each problem is interconnected with all the other problems in the world. In actual fact, the environment in which we live, in which all creatures live, is an environment that is nearly factorable into separate problems. Sometimes you're hungry, sometimes you're sleepy, sometimes you're cold. Fortunately, you're not often all three at the same time. Or if you are, all but one of these needs can be postponed until the most pressing is taken care of. You have lots of other needs, too, but these also do not all impinge on you at once.

We live in what might be called a nearly empty world—one in which there are millions of variables that in principle could affect each other but that most of the time don't. In gravitational theory everything is pulling at everything else, but some things pull harder than others, either because they're bigger or because they're closer. Perhaps there is actually a very dense network of interconnections in the world, but in most of the situations we face we can detect only a modest number of variables or considerations that dominate.

If this factorability is not wholly descriptive of the world we live in today—and I will express some reservations about that—it certainly describes the world in which human rationality evolved: the world of the cavemen's ancestors, and of the cavemen themselves. In that world, very little was happening most of the time, but periodically action had to be taken to deal with hunger, or to flee danger, or to secure protection against the coming winter. Rationality could focus on dealing with one or a few problems at a time, with the expectation that when other problems arose there would be time to deal with those too.[6]

Mechanisms for Bounded Rationality

What characteristics does an organism need to enable it to exercise a sensible kind of bounded reality? It needs

---

[6] A simple formal model of such rationality is provided by my "Rational Choice and the Structure of the Environment," *Psychological Review* 63: 129–38 (1956).

some way of focusing attention—of avoiding distraction (or at least too much distraction) and focusing on the things that need attention at a given time. A very strong case can be made, and has been made by physiological psychologists, that focusing attention is one of the principal functions of the processes we call emotions. One thing an emotion can do for and to you is to distract you from your current focus of thought, and to call your attention to something else that presumably needs attention right now. Most of the time in our society we don't have to be out looking for food, but every so often we need to be reminded that food is necessary. So we possess some mechanisms that arouse periodically the feeling of hunger, to direct our attention to the need for food. A similar account can be given of other emotions.

Some of an organism's requirements call for continuous activity. People need to have air—access to it can be interrupted only for a short time—and their blood must circulate continually to all parts of their bodies. Of course, human physiology takes care of these and other short-term insistent needs in parallel with the long-term needs. We do not have to have our attention directed to a lack of oxygen in our bloodstream in order to take a breath, or for our heart to beat. But by and large, with respect to those needs that are intermittent, that aren't constantly with us, we operate very much as serial, one-at-a-time, animals. One such need is about as many as our minds can handle at one time. Our ability to get away with that limitation, and to survive in spite of our seriality, depends on the mechanisms, particularly emotional mechanisms, that assure new problems of high urgency a high priority on the agenda.

Second, we need a mechanism capable of generating alternatives. A large part of our problem solving consists in the search for good alternatives, or for improvements in alternatives that we already know. In the past 25 years, research in cognitive psychology and artificial intelligence has taught us a lot about how alternatives are generated. I have given a description of some of the mechanisms in Chapters 3 and 4 of *The Sciences of the Artificial*.[7]

Third, we need a capability for acquiring facts about the environment in which we find ourselves, and a modest capability for drawing inferences from these facts. Of course, this capability is used to help generate alternatives as well as to assess their probable consequences, enabling the organism to maintain a very simple model of the part of the world that is relevant to its current decisions, and to do commonsense reasoning about the model.

What can we say for and about this behavioral version, this bounded rationality version, of human thinking and problem solving? The first thing we can say is that there is now a tremendous weight of evidence that this theory describes the way people, in fact, make decisions and solve problems. The theory has an increasingly firm empirical base as a description of human behavior. Second, it is a theory that accounts for the fact that creatures stay alive and even thrive, who—however smart they are or think they are—have modest computational abilities in comparison with the complexity of the entire world that surrounds them. It explains how such creatures have survived for at least the millions of years that our species has survived. In a world that is nearly empty, in which not every-

---

[7] Second ed. (Cambridge, Mass., 1981).

thing is closely connected with everything else, in which problems can be decomposed into their components—in such a world, the kind of rationality I've been describing gets us by.

Consequences of Bounded Rationality

Rationality of the sort described by the behavioral model doesn't optimize, of course. Nor does it even guarantee that our decisions will be consistent. As a matter of fact, it is very easy to show that choices made by an organism having these characteristics will often depend on the order in which alternatives are presented. If A is presented before B, A may seem desirable or at least satisfactory; but if B is presented before A, B will seem desirable and will be chosen before A is even considered.

The behavioral model gives up many of the beautiful formal properties of the Olympian model, but in return for giving them up it provides a way of looking at rationality that explains how creatures with our mental capacities—or even, with our mental capacities supplemented with all the computers in Silicon Valley—get along in a world that is much too complicated to be understood from the Olympian viewpoint of SEU theory.

INTUITIVE RATIONALITY

A third model of human rationality has been much less discussed by social scientists than the two that I've considered so far, but is perhaps even more prominent in the popular imagination. I've referred to it as the intuitive model. The intuitive model postulates that a great deal of human thinking, and a great deal of the success of human beings in arriving at correct decisions, is due to the fact that they have good intuition or good judgment. The notions of intuition and judgment are particularly prominent in public discussion today because of the research of Roger Sperry and others, much supplemented by speculation, on the specialization of the left and right hemispheres of the human brain.

The Two Sides of the Brain

In the minds and hands of some writers, the notion of hemisphere specialization has been turned into a kind of romance. According to this romanticized account, there's the dull, pedestrian left side of the brain, which is very analytic. It either, depending on your beliefs, does the Olympian kind of reasoning that I described first, or—if it's just a poor man's left hemisphere—does the behavioral kind of thinking I described as the second model. In either case, it's a down-to-earth, pedestrian sort of hemisphere, capable perhaps of deep analysis but not of flights of fancy. Then there's the right hemisphere, in which is stored human imagination, creativity—all those good things that account for the abilities of human beings, if they would entrust themselves to this hemisphere, to solve problems in a creative way.

Before I try to characterize intuition and creativity (they are not always the same thing) in a positive way, I must comment on the romantic view I have just caricatured. When we look for the empirical evidence for it, we find that there is none. There is lots of evidence, of course, for specialization of the hemispheres, but none of that evidence really argues that any complex human mental function is performed by either of the hemispheres alone under normal circumstances. By and large, the evidence shows that any kind of complex thinking that involves taking in information, processing that information, and doing something with it employs both of our hemispheres in varying proportions and in various ways.

Of course, brain localization is not the important issue at stake. Regardless of whether the same things or different things go on in the two hemispheres, the important question is whether there are two radically different forms of human thought—analytic thought and intuitive thought—and whether what we call creativity relies largely on the latter.

Intuition and Recognition

What is intuition all about? It is an observable fact that people sometimes reach solutions to problems suddenly. They then have an "aha!" experience of varying degrees of intensity. There is no doubt of the genuineness of the phenomenon. Moreover, the problem solutions people reach when they have these experiences, when they make intuitive judgments, frequently are correct.

Good data are available on this point for chess masters. Show a chess position, from a mid-game situation in a reasonable game, to a master or grand master. After looking at it for only five or ten seconds, he will usually be able to propose a strong move—very often the move that is objectively best in the position. If he's playing the game against a strong opponent, he won't make that move immediately; he may sit for three minutes or half an hour in order to decide whether or not his first intuition is really correct. But perhaps 80 or 90 percent of the time, his first impulse will in fact show him the correct move.

The explanation for the chess master's sound intuitions

is well known to psychologists, and is not really surprising.[8] It is no deeper than the explanation of your ability, in a matter of seconds, to recognize one of your friends whom you meet on the path tomorrow as you are going to class. Unless you are very deep in thought as you walk, the recognition will be immediate and reliable. Now in any field in which we have gained considerable experience, we have acquired a large number of "friends"—a large number of stimuli that we can recognize immediately. We can sort the stimulus in whatever sorting net performs this function in the brain (the physiology of it is not understood), and discriminate it from all the other stimuli we might encounter. We can do this not only with faces, but with words in our native language.

Almost every college-educated person can discriminate among, and recall the meanings of, fifty to a hundred thousand different words. Somehow, over the years, we have all spent many hundreds of hours looking at words, and we have made friends with fifty or a hundred thousand of them. Every professional entomologist has a comparable ability to discriminate among the insects he sees, and every botanist among the plants. In any field of expertise, possession of an elaborate discrimination net that permits recognition of any one of tens of thousands of different objects or situations is one of the basic tools of the expert and the principal source of his intuitions.

Counts have been made of the numbers of "friends" that chess masters have: the numbers of different configurations of pieces on a chessboard that are old familiar

---

[8] For a survey of the evidence, see my *Models of Thought* (New Haven, Conn., 1979), chaps. 6.2–6.5.

acquaintances to them. The estimates come out, as an order of magnitude, around fifty thousand, roughly comparable to vocabulary estimates for native speakers. Intuition is the ability to recognize a friend and to retrieve from memory all the things you've learned about the friend in the years that you've known him. And of course if you know a lot about the friend, you'll be able to make good judgments about him. Should you lend him money or not? Will you get it back if you do? If you know the friend well, you can say "yes" or "no" intuitively.

Acquiring Intuitions and Judgment

Why should we believe that the recognition mechanism explains most of the "aha!" experiences that have been reported in the literature of creativity? An important reason is that valid "aha!" experiences happen only to people who possess the appropriate knowledge. Poincaré rightly said that inspiration comes only to the prepared mind. Today we even have some data that indicate how long it takes to prepare a mind for world-class creative performance.

At first blush, it is not clear why it should take just as long in one field as in another to reach a world-class level of performance. However, human quality of performance is evaluated by comparing it with the performance of other human beings. Hence the length of human life is a controlling parameter in the competition; we can spend a substantial fraction of our lives, but no more, in increasing our proficiency. For this reason, the time required to prepare for world-class performance (by the people whose talents allow them to aspire to that level) should be roughly the same for different fields of activity.

Empirical data gathered by my colleague John R. Hayes for chess masters and composers, and somewhat less systematically for painters and mathematicians, indicate that ten years is the magic number. Almost no person in these disciplines has produced world-class performances without having first put in at least ten years of intensive learning and practice.

What about child prodigies? Mozart was composing world-class music perhaps by the time he was seventeen—certainly no earlier. (The standard Hayes used for music is five or more appearances of recordings of a piece of music in the Schwann catalog. Except for some Mozart juvenilia, which no one would bother to listen to if they hadn't been written by Mozart, there is no world-class Mozart before the age of seventeen.) Of course Mozart was already composing at the age of four, so that by age seventeen he had already been educating himself for thirteen years. Mozart is typical of the child prodigies whose biographies Hayes has examined. A *sine qua non* for outstanding work is diligent attention to the field over a decade or more.

Summary: The Intuitive and Behavioral Models

There is no contradiction between the intuitive model of thinking and the behavioral model, nor do the two models represent alternative modes of thought residing in different cerebral hemispheres and competing for control over the mind. All serious thinking calls on both modes, both search-like processes and the sudden recognition of familiar patterns. Without recognition based on previous experience, search through complex spaces would proceed in snail-like fashion. Intuition exploits the knowledge we have gained through our past searches. Hence we would expect what in fact occurs, that the expert will often be able to proceed intuitively in attacking a problem that requires painful search for the novice. And we would expect also that in most problem situations combining aspects of novelty with familiar components, intuition and search will cooperate in reaching solutions.

INTUITION AND EMOTION

Thus far in our discussion of intuitive processes we have left aside one of the important characteristics these processes are said to possess: their frequent association with emotion. The searching, plodding stages of problem solving tend to be relatively free from intense emotion; they may be described as cold cognition. But sudden discovery, the "aha!" experience, tends to evoke emotion; it is hot cognition. Sometimes ideas come to people when they are excited about something.

Emotion and Attention

Hence, in order to have anything like a complete theory of human rationality, we have to understand what role emotion plays in it. Most likely it serves several quite distinct functions. First of all, some kinds of emotion (e.g., pleasure) are consumption goods. They enter into the utility function of the Olympian theory, and must be counted among the goals we strive for in the behavioral model of rationality.

But for our purposes, emotion has particular importance because of its function of selecting particular things in our environments as the focus of our attention. Why

29

was Rachel Carson's *Silent Spring* so influential? The problems she described were already known to ecologists and the other biologists at the time she described them. But she described them in a way that aroused emotion, that riveted our attention on the problem she raised. That emotion, once aroused, wouldn't let us go off and worry about other problems until something had been done about this one. At the very least, emotion kept the problem in the back of our minds as a nagging issue that wouldn't go away.

In the Olympian model, all problems are permanently and simultaneously on the agenda (until they are solved). In the behavioral model, by contrast, the choice of problems for the agenda is a matter of central importance, and emotion may play a large role in that choice.

Emotion does not always direct our attention to goals we regard as desirable. If I may go back to my example of *Mein Kampf,* we observed that the reasoning in that book is not cold reasoning but hot reasoning. It is reasoning that seeks deliberately to arouse strong emotions, often the emotion of hate, a powerful human emotion. And of course, the influence of *Mein Kampf,* like that of *Silent Spring* or Picasso's *Guernica,* was due in large part to the fact that it did have evocative power, the ability to arouse and fix the attention of its German readers on the particular goals it had in mind.

A behavioral theory of rationality, with its concern for the focus of attention as a major determinant of choice, does not dissociate emotion from human thought, nor does it in any respect underestimate the powerful effects of emotion in setting the agenda for human problem solving.

Emotion in Education

I would like to take a brief excursion at this point in order to consider the role of emotion in education. If literary and artistic works have a considerable power to evoke emotions, as they certainly do, does this power suggest any special role for them in the educational process?

We all know that the humanities feel a bit besieged today. A large proportion of the students in our universities appear to want to enroll in law, business, or medicine, and the humanities suffer neglect, benign or otherwise. One argument that is often advanced by those who would counter this trend is that it may be better, more effective, for students to learn about the human condition by exposure to the artist's and humanist's view of the world than by exposure to the scientist's. Of course my own professional identifications put me on the other side of the argument, but I think we should look at the issue quite carefully. What are the optimum conditions for efficient human learning about central and important matters? Which is better, cold cognition or hot? And whichever is better, will we find that this is the kind we associate with the sciences or the humanities?

I should say here that I have heard physicists argue for a strong infusion of hot cognition in teaching their subject. The problems that excite them, and motivate them to understand rather abstruse matters, are the cosmological and philosophical problems associated with the fundamental particles, and with astrophysics and the architecture of the universe. So perhaps I should not have associated science strictly with cold cognition.

But let me go to a domain where the point can be made more unequivocally and convincingly. Perhaps some of you are familiar with Arthur Koestler's *Darkness at Noon*. It is a novel that describes what happens to a particular person at the time of the Russian purge trials of the 1930's. Now suppose you wish to understand the history of the Western world between the two world wars, and the events that led up to our contemporary world. You will then certainly need to understand the purge trials. Are you more likely to gain such an understanding by reading *Darkness at Noon*, or by reading a history book that deals with the trials, or by searching out the published transcripts of the trial testimony in the library? I would vote for Koestler's book as the best route, precisely because of the intense emotions it evokes in most readers.

I could go down a long list of such alternatives: *War and Peace* versus a treatise on military sociology, Proust and Chekov versus a textbook on personality. If I were in a position where I had to defend the role of the humanities in education, to provide an argument for something like the traditional liberal arts curriculum of the early twentieth century, I would argue for them on the grounds that most human beings are able to attend to issues longer, to think harder about them, to receive deeper impressions that last longer, if information is presented in a context of emotion—a sort of hot dressing—than if it is presented wholly without affect.

But educating with the help of hot cognition also implies a responsibility. If we are to learn our social science from novelists, then the novelists have to get it right. The scientific content must be valid. Freudian theory permeates a great deal of literature today—at the very time when Freudian theories are being revised radically by new psychological knowledge. There are few orthodox Freudians left in psychology today. Hence there is a danger, if we take this route of asking the humanities to provide an emotional context for learning, that a kind of warmed-over Freud will be served to our students in a powerfully influential form. We have to re-evaluate the great humanist classics to see to what extent they suffer from obsolescence through the progress of our scientific knowledge.

Homer is still alive because the *Iliad* and the *Odyssey* treat mainly of matters in which modern social science has not progressed much beyond lay understanding. Aristotle is barely alive—and certainly his scientific works are not, and his logic hardly. And we could have a great argument with philosophers as to whether his epistemology or his metaphysics has anything to say to students today. And Lucretius, of course, talking about atoms, has gone entirely.

The moral I draw is that, whereas works capable of evoking emotion may have special value for us just by virtue of that capability, if we wish to use them to educate, we must evaluate not only their power to rouse emotion but also their scientific validity when they speak of matters of fact.

If the humanities are to base their claims to a central place in the liberal curriculum on their special insights into the human condition, they must be able to show that their picture of that condition is biologically, sociologically, and psychologically defensible. It is not enough, for this particular purpose, that humanistic works move students.

They must move them in ways that will enable them to live with due regard for reason and fact in the real world. I do not mean to imply that the humanities do not now meet this standard; a detailed assessment of the liberal curriculum in any existing university would certainly not give a simple yes-or-no answer to that question. But I do suggest that any examination of the appropriate roles of different fields of knowledge in providing the materials of a liberal education needs to give close attention both to the emotional temperature of material and to its empirical soundness.

CONCLUSION

In this first chapter, I have sought to present three visions of rationality: three ways of talking about rational choice. The first of these, the Olympian model, postulates a heroic man making comprehensive choices in an integrated universe. The Olympian view serves, perhaps, as a model of the mind of God, but certainly not as a model of the mind of man. I have been rather critical of that theory for present purposes.

The second, the behavioral model, postulates that human rationality is very limited, very much bounded by the situation and by human computational powers. I have argued that there is a great deal of empirical evidence supporting this kind of theory as a valid description of how human beings make decisions. It is a theory of how organisms, including man, possessing limited computational abilities, make adaptive choices and sometimes survive in a complex, but mostly empty, world.

The third, the intuitive model, places great stress on the

processes of intuition. The intuitive theory, I have argued, is in fact a component of the behavioral theory. It emphasizes the recognition processes that underlie the skills humans can acquire by storing experience and by recognizing situations in which their experience is relevant and appropriate. The intuitive theory recognizes that human thought is often affected by emotion, and addresses the question of what function emotion plays in focusing human attention on particular problems at particular times.

I have left for the next chapter a fourth theory: the vision of rationality as evolutionary adaptation. The evolutionary model is a *de facto* model of rationality; it implies that only those organisms that adapt, that behave *as if* they were rational, will survive. In the next chapter, I shall examine these claims of the efficacy and centrality of natural selection as applied to the exercise of human rationality.

2. Rationality and Teleology

THE PREVIOUS chapter, in which I examined three alternative conceptions of rationality, focused not so much on the rational choices themselves, as on the *processes* for arriving at them. It was concerned with the processes of thinking that underlie judgment and choice, and with the differences between the models of the decision-making process that have been proposed over the years by people interested in rationality.

EVOLUTION VIEWED AS RATIONAL ADAPTATION

It is this view of rationality—from the standpoint of its results—that has been most prominent in evolutionary theories. Evolutionary theories explain the way things are by showing that this is the way they have to be in order for the organism to survive. *How* the organism achieves its well-adapted state is a matter of scientific interest, too, but from an evolutionary point of view it is secondary to the basic fact of adaptation or survival. So long as attention is directed to results, such a theory of rationality is compatible with an Olympian process, a behavioral one, or even an intuitive one.

Thus, it can be thought rational that birds build their

nests in trees, for that location helps protect eggs and young from earthbound predators. There is no implication in this way of speaking that the parent birds went through a process of decision—Olympian, behavioral, or intuitive—to arrive at this choice of location. Nest-building is simply an instinctual behavior, a highly adaptive one that has been selected from other, less adaptive ones through the processes of evolution. It is in this sense that the outcome of evolutionary processes may be regarded as a form of rationality, and indeed as an alternative to the forms we considered in the last chapter.

"As-if" Theories of Adaptation

One reason for being interested in evolutionary approaches to, and interpretations of, rationality, is that some social scientists, and particularly some economists, have argued that it isn't important to know *how* people go about making decisions. It isn't important because we know, from the fact that they have survived, that they did in fact make rational, adaptive decisions.

Milton Friedman takes this point of view in his well-known essays on methodology.[1] There he argues for an "as-if" theory of economic behavior: a theory that businessmen and business firms behave *as if* they had made the correct, rational calculations that would be required to achieve, let's say, a maximum of utility or profit. The ground for the argument is that only those who succeed in maximizing stay in business; the others have disappeared from the scene. All that matters in this view are results—success in adapting to the economic environ-

[1] Milton Friedman, *Essays in Positive Economics* (Chicago, 1953).

ment. It does not matter at all what process of ratiocination—or what random process, for that matter—achieved the adaptation.

This answer won't satisfy us fully if our curiosity about how the world works extends beyond a concern for the public policy implications of business firm behavior. Even if we knew, or believed, that only those survived who acted as if they were making rational calculations, we would still wonder just what the survivors did to survive. Perhaps miracles and spectacular coincidences do occur constantly in this world; but perhaps also there is some underlying mechanism that governs survival. Understanding the mechanism, we would be in a better position to judge how likely it would be to keep the evolving system in the neighborhood of its equilibrium, and whether deviations from equilibrium would likely be sufficiently great to affect policy significantly.

Variation and Selection

The as-if answer won't satisfy us either unless we can be sure that the equilibrium arrived at is unique. If different processes would lead us to different equilibria, a result that we shall see is likely, then process again acquires a central role both in understanding the phenomena and in drawing out their implications for policy.

In modern Darwinian biological theories of evolution, for all their emphasis on the result (i.e., survival), there is assumed, of course, not a miracle but a mechanism—or, more precisely, a combination of at least two mechanisms. These are *variation*, which creates new forms of life, and *selection*, which preserves forms that are well adapted to their environments.[2] There are some interesting parallels between these Darwinian mechanisms and the mechanisms I described in the last chapter as underlying a behavioral theory of rationality.

According to the behavioral theory, rational choice may require a great deal of selective search in order to discover adaptive responses. The simplest, most primitive search processes require that possible responses be first generated and then tested for appropriateness. The generator-test mechanism is the direct analogue, in the behavioral theory of rationality, of the variation-selection mechanism of the Darwinian theory. Just as in biological evolution we have variation to produce new organisms, so in the behavioral theory of human rationality we have some kind of generation of alternatives—some kind of combinatorial process that can take simple ideas and put them together in new ways. And similarly, just as in the biological theory of evolution the mechanism of natural selection weeds out poorly adapted variants, so in human thinking the testing process rejects ideas other than those that contribute to solving the problem that is being addressed.

Among psychologists, Donald T. Campbell has been most forceful in pointing out and developing this analogy between Darwinian evolution and behavioral rationality.[3]

[2] I use the term *variation* rather than *mutation* because mutation is only one of the Darwinian mechanisms (and perhaps not the most important) that create new forms. Two other mechanisms of variation in classical genetics are crossover of chromosome segments and inversion. But most fundamental of all is the basic reproduction cycle which, through meiosis and the fertilization of eggs by sperm, produces new sets of variant chromosome combinations at each generation. I will have more to say about these mechanisms presently.

[3] See, for example, D. T. Campbell, "Evolutionary Epistemology," in P. A. Schilpp, ed., *The Philosophy of Karl Popper* (La Salle, Ill., 1974), 1:413–63.

In economics, Richard Nelson and Sidney Winter have been similarly concerned with defining mechanisms that could account for the evolution and adaptation of business firms.[4] The "genes" of Nelson and Winter are the habits, routines, and standard operating procedures that firms employ in the conduct of their affairs. From time to time, new practices are devised, which then must prove themselves in the marketplace in competition with the old. The rationality supported by this process is also closely allied to behavioral rationality, for there is no guarantee that the system will ever arrive at, or approach, a position of optimality. It is adaptive, but not necessarily optimizing.

A final preliminary remark: in applying evolutionary ideas to human societies, we need to be a little cautious about the theory's statistical assumptions. In our abstract model of selection of the fittest, we imagine that a number of models (variations) are produced and tested over a sequence of generations; one of them survives the processes of selection. But if we are to apply evolutionary ideas to contemporary society, we must ask whether statistical selection by repeated trials is feasible. How many nuclear explosions will it take to determine which species are fit enough to survive on the globe? Many of us think that one such explosion would be more than enough to settle this issue for the human species, and that there is little sense in applying the law of large numbers or notions of sequential testing to nuclear events.

Some kinds of experiments are difficult to carry out, therefore, on a statistical basis, because you can go

[4] R. R. Nelson and S. G. Winter, *Evolutionary Theory of Economic Change* (Cambridge, Mass., 1982).

through only one generation. If you envision evolution as a trial-and-error process in which the errors are weeded out by the forces of selection, this is an inappropriate model when there is only one trial and not room for even a single error. We need to keep that caution in mind as we apply evolutionary models to the future development of the human species and human society.

THE DARWINIAN MODEL

I have already mentioned the basic mechanisms that underlie the Darwinian model of evolution. The process of variation produces new forms, and the process of selection evaluates these forms and determines which shall survive. The standard literature on Darwinian evolution, and especially the formal literature, focuses on the concept called *fitness*. If two organisms are trying to live in the same ecological niche (i.e., are trying to make use of precisely the same resources), one of the two may produce, on average, more surviving progeny per adult than the other. The more prolific of the two organisms is the fitter. If its progeny continue to outcompete the other's, it will soon greatly outnumber the less fit organism and will eventually, because of total resource limitations, drive it to extinction.

Fitness

Central to the Darwinian theory, therefore, is the notion that fitness is all that counts. All that matters is whether an organism can outbreed its rivals, because the species that can occupy a given niche most efficiently (where efficiency is defined as fitness) is the one that will survive.

From our knowledge of how interest compounds, we can readily calculate that an organism with a fitness advantage over its competitor of only 1.05/1.00 per generation will have twice as many progeny as the competitor within fourteen generations. If, as seems to be the case, the human species evolved several million years ago, there have been about 100,000 generations in which superior fitness could assert itself. There have been only four or five hundred generations, of course, since our species shifted from a hunting to an agricultural mode of life, but even this span allows for an enormous amount of selection. Over 400 generations, a 1.05/1.00 fitness advantage would yield a 250,000/1 superiority in number of progeny. Even a 1.01/1.00 advantage would yield a 13/1 superiority.

On the other hand, if we think that modern industrial society confronts humankind with very different conditions for success and survival from those of agricultural society, then there have been less than a dozen generations (at the most generous estimate) on which the new conditions could act—hardly enough to bring about substantial selection. In any event, when we talk of the effect of selection forces on our species, we must specify which part of its history we are considering: the long ages of its early development under very primitive conditions, the thousands of years of human agricultural society, or the scant two centuries of modern society. Our estimates of the consequences of evolutionary pressure will depend very much on how far we think the newer conditions differ from the older with respect to which characteristics may be adaptive.

From this way of conceptualizing survival of the fittest comes the idea of the selfish gene. A gene cannot afford to do anything (if we may anthropomorphize a bit about genes) except to be as fit as it can be. Any other course will diminish its chances of survival. Hence an altruistic gene, a gene that looks out for the welfare of others at the expense of its own fitness, is an anomaly not likely to be encountered in nature except under rather unusual circumstances, which I shall discuss presently. The central mechanism in this model is the competition for niches.

Niche Elaboration

The empirical study of evolutionary processes, both in the field and in the laboratory, is largely devoted to understanding the competition for niches. The theory of niche competition has another aspect, however, besides a brute-force struggle for occupancy, an aspect that is sometimes associated with the name of Durkheim[5] but can also be found in *The Origin of Species*. The alternative view starts with the observation that there are two ways in which a creature can seek to survive in a jungle environment. One way is to compete fiercely and successfully for an existing niche with other creatures that are trying to occupy it. The other way is to find a wholly unoccupied niche, or to alter and specialize itself in order to be able to occupy efficiently (fitly) a niche that is not now occupied effectively by anyone else.

One can conceive of a system in which large numbers of different kinds of organisms coexist because the system of niches has proliferated to provide each organism with its own little cranny, with perhaps additional niches remain-

[5] Emile Durkheim, *The Division of Labor in Society* (Glencoe, Ill., 1947), Book II, chap. 2.

ing at least temporarily unoccupied or occupied only inefficiently by organisms not specially adapted to them. One form that this proliferation takes, which has been observed in the study of island populations of closely related species, is the substitution of two specialized forms for a single generalized form (say, one large and one small species where there had been a single species of intermediate size). Each of the two more specialized forms may be more efficient than the single "all-purpose" form in harvesting a particular part of the food range. The smaller variety typically exploits smaller prey, the larger variety larger prey. The specialists might be independently introduced into the biota, or they could emerge by variation and natural selection from the original single form.

The theory of niche elaboration has not been as fully developed in the literature of population genetics as the theory of competition among organisms for single niches.[6] The former theory is likely to be considerably more complicated than the latter, since it must explain the proliferation of niches as well as the proliferation of organisms to fill them. Moreover, an important part of each organism's environment in such a system is provided by the other organisms that surround it. The very creation of niches, and the eventual development of new creatures to fill them, alters the system in such a way as to allow the development of still more niches.

Before fleas could evolve and survive, there had to be dogs to provide a niche in which fleas could live. Before

[6] But see G. E. Hutchinson, *The Ecological Theater and the Evolutionary Play* (New Haven, Conn., 1965), pp. 26–78; and E. Mayr, *Animal Species and Evolution* (Cambridge, Mass., 1965), pp. 87–88.

any animals whatever could evolve, there had to be plants that could serve as food and there had to be niches for those plants to fill. Consequently, there seem to be two quite different directions that evolutionary theory can take. A more restricted form of the theory can focus, as the classical theory has, on fitness—on the problem of competition for a single niche or a fixed system of niches. But there is need for a much broader theory, in which the system of niches itself changes and develops simultaneously with the development of the niche-filling creatures. This latter theory is in a very early stage of development.

There are at least two different ways, then, not necessarily mutually exclusive, to explain the large number of distinct species—of the order of several millions—that now inhabit the earth. First, because of variations in topography and climate, there might exist hundreds of millions of distinct microenvironments (niches) to which species could separately adapt, and these niches may have been filled gradually as the processes of variation continued to create new kinds of organisms. The niches could have long pre-existed the species that now fill them, and there may remain vast numbers of niches that are unoccupied or occupied at a relatively low level of fitness by organisms not efficiently specialized to suit them.

The alternative picture begins with a largely inorganic earth offering a more limited range of different microenvironments, and it envisions a process whereby new environments, and new differences among environments, are constantly created as new species come into being. If this alternative picture is valid, or even partially valid, the proliferation of species may continue indefinitely; whereas if the picture of a fixed supply of niches is valid, we would expect the evolution of new, fitter species sooner or later to require the obliteration of older, less fit ones.

The evidence on this point is conflicting. On the one hand, it has been said that more than 99 percent of all species that have existed are now extinct. On the other hand, numerous species exist today that are found, in essentially identical form or very similar form, in fossil records from hundreds of millions of years ago. (This fact was once thought to score heavily against Darwinism.) One can say that some species established their fitness very early, a fitness that has never been successfully challenged; but that these offered no barrier to the emergence of large numbers of new species that found new and unoccupied niches. These facts provide a very different picture of evolutionary history from the naïve "struggle for existence."

Variation

What Darwin proposed was a selection mechanism for evolution. He did not propose a specific mechanism for producing variation, and indeed our understanding of how variation comes about is still quite incomplete. Fitness tells us why better organisms, once created, survive, but it gives no hint of the origin of superior organisms that can take part in the competitive process. Yet without a source of candidates, the process could not work.

The discovery of chromosomes and their recombination by meiosis in each generation (at least in sexually reproducing organisms) provided scientists with a possible mechanism for generating new forms. However, with twenty chromosome pairs (and few organisms have more), each existing in two allelic forms, with dominance only 2^{20}, about one million, different variants could be generated. A million is not a large enough number to account for major organismic evolution over any considerable period of time. Nature would soon run out of possibilities.

The further discovery of the multiplicity of genes within chromosomes, and of the mutation of individual genes, vastly increased the range of variation possible. However, mutation is a relatively rare event and most mutations are not adaptive. Biologists have long doubted that mutation by itself was a sufficiently powerful mechanism to account for variation.

A third discovery was even more significant: that chromosomes do not recombine exclusively as units. Instead, a great deal of recombination takes place even among the genes in a single chromosome, through crossing-over, inversion, and other restructuring processes. This recombination can be quite radical, involving, for example, the duplication or elimination of whole segments of DNA. The fact of micro-recombination once again enormously increases the possibilities for variation. Complex organisms typically carry at least 10,000 genes (it may be as many as 100,000) in their chromosomes. Now, if each gene existed in two alleles, $2^{10,000} = 10^{3,000}$ different organisms could be produced. All of geological time would not even begin to suffice to explore this whole space of potential organisms—or even a small part of it. Moreover, recombinations do not take place rarely, as mutations do; some (e.g., crossing-over) take place frequently and in every cell division by meiosis.

Hence, even without frequent mutation, the modifications of DNA produced in the normal course of cell division and reproduction would seemingly provide adequate variation to account for the many organismic forms that have appeared in the course of evolution. Moreover, since under these circumstances, only a tiny fraction of the genetically potential organisms will ever actually emerge from the combinatorial process and be tested for their fitness, we should henceforth speak of the survival of the fitter rather than the survival of the fittest. There would seem to be no permanent equilibrium of species, since new effective competitors can arise from the reproductive process at any time and the vast majority of potential competitors have never been generated (and never will be). This is a further reason why population genetics needs to attend to the dynamic processes that generate species, and not just to the results of the struggle among existing forms for occupation of niches.

Phenotype and Genotype

The forms and behaviors of organisms, the phenotypes, are produced under the strong influence of the underlying genetic structures, the genotypes. But the mapping between genotypes and phenotypes is complicated. Natural selection operates on the phenotypes; it is they who compete in the environment. Genetic change operates on the genotypes. All the evidence rejects Lamarckian claims that the experiences or modifications of a phenotype can act directly to modify its genotype. Natural selection, which modifies genotype frequencies by causing differential rates of reproduction of different phenotypes, is the only linkage between the

49

two. Parents who have learned algebra do not, alas, increase by their experience the algebraic aptitude of their progeny.

A single phenotypic trait—height, for example—may be influenced by a number of different genes; conversely, a single gene may influence the development of various traits. Furthermore, a particular favorable value of a trait may be attained, by different members of a species, through different allele combinations. We cannot assume in a human population that all persons of a given height have the same combination of alleles for controlling height. There may be a substantial number of alternative genetic patterns that, holding environment constant, would produce people of the same height.

This kind of genetic diversity must be especially characteristic of complex, heterogeneous traits like "intelligence." Natural selection may have, and probably has, produced many alternative genetic foundations for human intelligent behavior. Some of the genetic variety may show up in differential abilities on distinct tasks requiring intelligence for their performance; but in other cases similar capabilities may rest on different genetic foundations. For example, the capacity and persistence of short-term memory plays an important role in most cognitive tasks. Quite different genetic patterns might produce short-term memory structures of comparable effectiveness.

In the human species, more than any other, the phenotypic variations that are of greatest importance for effective functioning tend to be very diffuse, rather than particularistic. Such general and heterogeneous qualities as health, strength, intelligence, dexterity, learning ability, and temperament are far more significant, for both biological fitness and the human condition, than more specific traits like eye color, cephalic index, or tendency to baldness. Hence, in the history of the human species, we would expect selective pressure to have been exerted most effectively on general qualities like those just listed. However, because of the heterogeneity of these qualities, we would not expect that pressure to have produced a high level of genetic uniformity.

Energy Utilization

We can also think of species filling niches as drawing on resources, and ultimately on the energy supplied by the sun. Perhaps the opportunities for the elaboration of niches and the proliferation of species are seriously limited by the total energy available to them. We must consider this possibility.

An important characteristic of living organisms is that they do not simply burn up energy (although they do that, too), but use energy at relatively high temperatures to build up their structures, thereby degrading the energy thermodynamically while converting some of it into organic tissue. Insofar as energy is converted to organized protoplasmic structure and not immediately metabolized, there is no limit to the inventory of such energy that living creatures can build up over a period of time. Eventually, as processes of death and decay balance the new additions to this inventory, an equilibrium is reached.

In the absence of living organisms, the solar energy received by the earth is degraded essentially in one step before being radiated again into space. Living organisms, by storing energy at intermediate levels, delay this process of degradation. The energy is reused, sometimes four or five times, as it progresses down the food chain from plants, through herbivores and various carnivores, to reducers (bacteria and the like). The amount of life that can be maintained by solar energy is largely determined by the efficiency of these processes: what proportion of the energy is captured for "inventory" rather than expended for metabolism, and how much the energy is degraded at each reuse.

Although photosynthesis may utilize as much as 10 or 12 percent of the directly incident radiation, vegetation seldom captures more than about 1 percent of the sun's total energy, the rest being absorbed in the atmosphere or reflected from the surface. A herbivore or carnivore may convert a substantial fraction of the energy contained in its food into its own structure and into the energy used in its own metabolism, but in view of the loss through metabolism, we can count on a degradation of usable energy by a factor of nearly ten at each step down the food chain. Nor, even with the possibilities for energy storage in vegetation and animal matter, are the recycling times long. The mean cycle time from the initial moment of photosynthesis through the final stage of organic degradation can hardly be more than ten or twenty years.[7]

These numbers indicate that there remain large opportunities for the more efficient exploitation of solar energy, hence that a deficiency in solar energy cannot be regarded as a serious limiting factor on continuing evolution.

[7] Data on the sizes of these flows and inventories may be found in E. P. Odum, *Fundamentals of Ecology*, 3d ed. (Philadelphia, 1971), chap. 3.

Moreover, although these figures give some quantitative measure of the total biomass the earth might support, they say nothing about the variety of niches that can exist or the variety of organisms that could occupy these niches. The most plausible hypothesis is that variety increases continuously to exploit the opportunities for specialization that are provided by the vast and increasing diversity of niches.

Darwin, inspired by Malthus's observation that unchecked population growth would be geometric, emphasized the limits of growth and the competition for fixed, scarce resources. But we have just seen that this is not the whole story. Evolution can produce new organisms capable of exploiting energy and other resources that were previously wasted or used inefficiently. And this has in fact happened as animal life came to occupy the new niches provided by plants, and as living forms extended their occupancy of the earth's environment from sea to land. One would suppose that, perhaps on a smaller scale, this kind of extension continues today. There is no reason to think that we are near to a stable equilibrium.

SOCIAL AND CULTURAL EVOLUTION

We have seen that human biological evolution spans some 100,000 generations, whereas evolution since the emergence of agriculture spans only perhaps 400 generations. During the latter period, we have little evidence of biological modification of our species, but enormous evidence of continuing cultural change. This has led some observers to hypothesize that cultural evolution has replaced genetic evolution as the principal process for continuing modification of our species. However, it is not entirely obvious how this hypothesis can be reconciled with a Darwinian model. In that model it is the *gene* that evolves, not the individual, much less a whole society.

In a system organized around the selfish gene, is there room for a notion of cultural evolution? The recent work of Lumsden and Wilson deals specifically with the problems of human culture in an evolutionary framework.[8] These authors juxtapose with the biological gene a cultural "gene" (*culturgen*) that can be transmitted, not biologically but socially, from one person in a culture to another, and from one generation to another. They argue that we can conceive of a culture as developing by means of a yoked process between a set of biological genes and a set of culturgens. The yoking of the two components implies that they must be compatible with each other. The culturgens most likely to be transmitted are those most easily perceived and used on the basis of the biological makeup of the members of that society. For example, the color vocabularies in languages reflect the color-sensing mechanisms of the human eye. Human biological characteristics exert strong influences on sexual behavior, infant care, and cognitive processes and strategies.[9]

Lumsden and Wilson point out that the reverse proposition also holds: the presence of certain culture traits (to call culturgens by their more usual name) in a society may change the fitness associated with particular biological

[8] C. J. Lumsden and E. O. Wilson, *Genes, Mind, and Culture* (Cambridge, Mass., 1981).

[9] That human biology strongly molds human behavior is hardly controversial. What is much more controversial, of course, is whether *differences* in individual biology account for *differences* in individual (or group) behavior, and if so to what extent.

genes. Hence a set of social organisms capable of transmitting a culture may undergo evolutionary processes that are a great deal more complex than the processes of organisms not capable of transmitting a culture. For there will be mutual interaction whereby the genetic material determines what kinds of culture traits can develop, while at the same time the culture traits that are present at any given moment are influencing the fitness and consequent survival of variations in the genes. The theory of this kind of interaction does not have a large literature today; Lumsden and Wilson are perhaps the first to treat of it at book length.

A species that can change its culture is "programmable." As suggested earlier, the kinds of genetic traits that could most effectively exploit the flexibility of behavior of a programmable species would be traits broadly applicable to a wide range of environments: traits conducive to strength, good health, dexterity, and, above all, the ability to think and learn. Programmability is also conducive to social existence and most effectively exploited in a social environment rather than an isolated one. In particular, let us examine a specially important aspect of programmability: susceptibility to accepting programs under social influence or pressure. I shall refer to this kind of susceptibility as "docility." We need not ask which is chicken and which egg—cognitive abilities and temperament adapted to social living, on the one hand, or human society as an adaptive mechanism, on the other. Clearly each reinforces the other, and in mutual interaction both contribute to fitness.

It is certainly plausible that under the conditions our species has experienced during most of its existence, both athletic prowess and intelligence contributed positively to its reproductive success, or fitness. The case has often been made, and hardly needs to be spelled out. It is less obvious that in recent human generations (say, the last hundred years in industrial society) there is any positive relation between these qualities and numbers of surviving progeny produced. The idea that the link may have been broken by recent cultural change is the basis for various policy proposals that go under the label of eugenics. I shall not address this difficult topic here. To contemplate a society interceding in the reproductive process to shape its own genetic constitution is not *a priori* foolish. But many complexities would have to be dealt with and many booby traps avoided before a satisfactory social policy to this end could be formulated.

If flexibility (as attained, say, through strength, dexterity, or intelligence) is the main route to fitness in a programmable social species, then the strong and the clever in such a species may have an advantage of fitness that is almost independent of the particular content of the culture. They will be the best able to adapt, whatever it is they are adapting to. Hence one can conceive of the culture evolving semi-independently of the species that supports it. The mechanisms for the inheritance of culture traits (especially various forms of individual and social imitation) are very different from the mechanisms of biological inheritance. Cultural inheritance is distinctly Lamarckian; acquired traits can indeed be transmitted.

There are at least two potential consequences of the weak linkage between the two evolutionary mechanisms. On the one hand, the successful spread of a collection of culture traits (e.g., Western industrialism) does not imply superior genetic fitness of the originators of those traits; they may multiply slowly or not at all, and can become a smaller and smaller part of the population bearing the culture they initially developed. On the other hand, if a particular human group has a culture that provides them with superior fitness in competition with other groups, then, so long as that culture does not impose self-defeating selection pressures on the group that possesses it, it may provide the basis for a genuine "social evolution," i.e., for the survival of this group at the expense of others. This can only happen, of course, if extensive borrowing by competing groups can be prevented. The European conquest of North America provides perhaps the clearest example of this process in modern times.

The history of human conquest illustrates how complex the relation is between the fitness of cultures and the genetic fitness of the culture bearers. The Mongols, in the thirteenth and fourteenth centuries, were highly successful in conquering a large part of the inhabited world of that time. This success did not imply, however, either cultural or genetic fitness. On the cultural side, they largely adopted the forms of the societies they conquered. On the genetic side, it is not at all clear that the numbers of Mongol peoples increased more rapidly (if they increased at all) than the numbers of the various peoples they conquered.

ALTRUISM IN EVOLUTIONARY PROCESSES

The term altruism can be construed in a number of different ways. The most restrictive concept is pure altruism or *strong altruism*: unrequited sacrifice of fitness for the benefit of other organisms. A broader concept, and the one in which we shall be particularly interested, is *weak altruism*, which we shall see means, essentially, *enlightened self-interest*. We speak of weak altruism when an individual sacrifices fitness in the short run but receives indirect long-run rewards that more than compensate for the immediate sacrifice. In recent years population geneticists have elucidated a number of mechanisms that can account for the evolution of weak altruism.[10] Each of these mechanisms depends on a particular kind of indirect pathway for the reward of the altruistic gene.

Mechanisms That Select for Altruism

To determine the minimal conditions under which weak altruism will survive, we describe two mechanisms for altruism that have been investigated: kinship and the structured deme.

Kinship models provide a much discussed mechanism of weak altruism. If individuals can recognize their close kin, then, since the kin carry many of the same genes as the altruistic individual, sacrifice that contributes to the survival of the kin can increase the fitness of these common genes. "Recognition" can consist, minimally, of simply living in close propinquity to the kin and providing special benefits to near neighbors—no specific ability to distinguish kin from strangers is required in this version of the model.

The kinship model is likely to work (i.e., to explain increased fitness) only if it produces differential effects on very close kin, for even first cousins have only one-eighth

---

[10] An excellent account of theories of altruism in population genetics will be found in D. S. Wilson, *The Natural Selection of Populations and Communities* (Menlo Park, Calif., 1980).

of their genes in common. Hence, the kinship mechanism has its greatest plausibility in explaining maternal nurturance of the young, sibling loyalty and sacrifice, and similar altruistic behaviors among members of the nuclear family. For the same reason, altruism based on kinship might be expected to occur more frequently with nonsexual than with sexual reproduction.

An important extension beyond kinship models of altruism is found in models based on the concept of a *structured deme*. We assume an area occupied by a population of organisms of a particular species, and we assume this entire population (the deme) to be divided into a number of local populations (trait groups). We suppose the life cycle of the species to be divided into two phases. During the first phase, individuals interact only with other individuals in the same trait group. During the second phase, the entire population of the deme mixes homogeneously before settling down again into newly constituted trait groups. For simplicity, we assume that reproduction and selection take place during the first phase only.

Now suppose mutation produces an altruistic gene that causes the altruistic individual to engage in some activity of benefit to all the members of its trait group (but not to other members of the deme), at some cost to itself. Within any given trait group, the result will be to increase the fitness of the nonaltruists relative to that of the altruist. However, there will be some variation, from one trait group to another, in the ratio of altruists to nonaltruists. Average fitness will be highest in those trait groups where there are the largest numbers of altruists (since the cost of its altruistic behavior to each altruist is more than compensated by the altruistic reward it receives from the large number of other altruists in the group). The altruists in these favored trait groups can have higher fitness than the nonaltruists in groups with higher numbers of nonaltruists. It is easy to show rigorously that if there is a sufficiently large variance in the proportion of altruists among the different trait groups, the average fitness of altruists will exceed the average fitness of nonaltruists, with the result that the altruistic gene will replace the nonaltruistic in the population. The variance required to produce this result is not excessive; in fact, if the altruists are distributed among the various trait groups with a variance as great as that of the binomial distribution, the altruistic gene will prevail.

There appear to be a number of systems like this in nature. By way of illustration, let me describe one discussed by D. S. Wilson.[11] There are certain species of insects that live in pitcher plants, where they find little pools of water in which they lay their eggs and raise their young. During one phase of the life cycle these insects live with a few others of their kind (the trait group) in a single isolated pitcher, and without interaction with the trait groups residing in other pitchers. Later the insects swarm over a much larger area (the deme), mixing more or less homogeneously with their cospecifics from all the trait groups prior to settling down again for reproduction in particular pitchers.

Suppose one of the insects in a particular pitcher plant undergoes a mutation leading to activities on its part that make life better for all the insects in the pitcher—it changes, for example, the acidity of the water, or adds

[11] *Ibid.*, pp. 21, 35–36.

some beneficial substance to it. If this activity costs energy that could otherwise be used to produce progeny, then the fitness of the mutant will be decreased while that of the nonaltruistic inhabitants of the same pitcher will be increased. Good guys do appear to finish last in this kind of world—but not, as we have seen, if there are different proportions of mutants in different plants. An accidental concentration of mutants in one pitcher can turn the advantage in favor of the mutant strain.

The apparent paradox in this result can be dispelled by noting that, on average, altruists will live in trait groups with a higher proportion of altruists than are present in the trait groups inhabited mostly by non-altruists. That is to say, on average, altruists will be exposed to a more benevolent environment in their trait groups than will non-altruists; hence the altruists will be fitter.[12]

In the structured deme model, the altruist receives his reward (hence is only a weak altruist) even though the only mechanism for selecting him out for reward is his residing in a neighborhood that may also be inhabited by other altruists. But it is precisely this localization that produces the "recognition" of altruists, and their consequent success. Without this differential return, the altruist would not survive.

Recognition of the Altruist

As soon as we introduce a wider range of mechanisms for identifying the altruist and rewarding him differen-

[12] The mechanism of the structured deme is analogous to Prisoner's Dilemma strategies described in the next chapter. For a discussion of the connection between the two concepts, see R. Axelrod and W. D. Hamilton, "The Evolution of Cooperation," *Science* 211: 1390–96 (March 27, 1981).

tially, the potential for the evolution of altruistic behaviors (still in this sense of enlightened self-interest) increases enormously. We then don't have to assume that the whole competition among a single species is simply a matter of tooth and claw, and we can give an explanation of why some nice people survive in the world. Human beings, and members of a number of other species as well, have a large ability to recognize individuals with whom they have previously interacted and to behave differentially toward them on the basis of what happened in past interactions.

Taking account of this ability, it is easy to construct models that will predict the coevolution of altruistic behaviors and the reciprocal behaviors of the recipients of altruism. In such an interacting society, changes in the behavior of any one organism toward the others can result in mutual reciprocal changes, and an evolution of niches can be brought about in this way. Thus the high degree of specialization that we actually observe in society has an obvious evolutionary explanation. Let us look more closely at how this may come about.

Altruism in Social Evolution

In a social environment, the particular behavior of any given individual may be rewarded or punished by its neighbors. In viewing society as a niche that may reward altruistic behavior and thereby modify genetic endowment in the direction of altruism, we must interpret "reward" in a very particular way. The only rewards that count for a Darwinian selection process are rewards that increase fitness. Showering riches or glory on people will have no genetic consequences unless the rich and famous are thereby enabled to produce more progeny than they otherwise would—that is, unless their rewards increase their ability to obtain spouses and to rear children, and their desire to do so.

In fact, the development of a genetic base for altruistic behavior would seem to call for the coevolution of three sets of traits: (1) a tendency to indicate by our behavior our approval of the altruistic behavior of others (or our disapproval of selfish behavior), (2) a tendency to respond to the expressed approval or disapproval of others by feeling guilt or shame, and (3) a tendency to reward altruism not only with approval but with opportunities (or responsibilities) for increased procreation.

All three traits are essential. In particular, altruism can only be expected to thrive genetically if it contributes to fitness. As remarked earlier, it is easier to see the connection between social approval and reproductive success in earlier societies than in our society today. Until recent times, however, that connection must have been strong, with withdrawal of social support not only barring access to spouses but generally endangering family survival. Hence, whether or not such selective pressures are exerted in contemporary societies, there has been no lack of time for the development of genetic traits of human responsiveness to social pressure, and of the propensity of humans to exert such pressure on each other.

However, as we have seen, many of society's rewards to individuals (and punishments as well) have no relation at all to fitness. Provided the members of the society, for whatever evolutionary reasons, value these rewards, they can be used to induce socially approved behavior, includ-

63

ing behavior usually regarded as "altruistic." Suppose, for example, that in a particular society the wealthy do not produce more progeny than the poor. Now the desire of wealthy people for esteem may lead them to part with their wealth for charitable purposes, a behavior usually regarded as altruistic. But as long as charitable giving does not affect genetic fitness, it is not, from an evolutionary point of view, a genetically altruistic behavior.

Hence sociology defines altruism much more broadly than does genetics, and social rewards may support many kinds of socially altruistic behavior that are genetically neutral. Of course, in any theory that assumes human behavior is motivated, this altruism can always be interpreted as reciprocal or weak, rather than strong, altruism. The rich man gives money but receives acclaim. Nevertheless, one does not need to demonstrate that, on average, his fitness has been increased to reconcile his socially altruistic behavior with the doctrine of natural selection. The long-term survival of the behavior may be determined by the fact that it contributes to the fitness of the whole society, hence is rewarded by the society.

To be sure, in a still longer run, motives like the desire for acclaim would be supported by natural selection only if they contributed, on average, to individual fitness. But notice that the linkage is not directly between acclaim and altruism, but between acclaim and *whatever behavior the society wishes to acclaim*. Responsiveness to acclaim is one important form of the more general trait I previously called docility. Let me turn specifically, then, to docility as a basis for altruism.

Docility may be defined as the propensity to behave in socially approved ways and to refrain from behaving in ways that are disapproved. Docility, like any other trait, is presumably developed under the influence of the processes of natural selection. That is, the level of docility will tend to rise if docility contributes positively to individual fitness, and to decline if it damages fitness.[13] Remember, though, that docility is a propensity to behave not in specific ways but in ways defined as appropriate by the society. Hence some of the behaviors imposed on the individual by this mechanism may increase his fitness; others may decrease it. If his docility becomes too selective—accepting only demands that increase his fitness—it is no longer docility, hence will not receive the social rewards that are given for docility.

Docility undoubtedly enhances human fitness tremendously by allowing children to enjoy a long period of dependence, and to acquire effective skills through learning. It may also, of course, cause children and others to engage in altruistic behaviors that do not increase their fitness. On average, however, the contribution to fitness of a relatively high level of docility must be positive.

We can, then, without contradicting the doctrine of the "selfish gene," introduce mechanisms for the evolutionary change of an entire society that impose *social* criteria on the selection process. What is required is that reward become linked to a generalized set of docile or "obeying" behav-

[13] Compare the discussion of flexibility and indoctrinability in E. O. Wilson, *Sociobiology* (Cambridge, Mass., 1975). See also D. T. Campbell, "On the Genetics of Altruism and the Counterhedonic Components of Human Culture," *Journal of Social Issues* 28 (3): 21–37 (1972).

iors rather than to specific behaviors. All that is required of these mechanisms is that they contribute *on balance* to individual fitness. There is no requirement that each of the specific behaviors they enjoin make such a contribution.

As we know from the existence of social insects, there are other foundations than this one for the evolution of social dependence. However, human social behavior is peculiarly intertwined with the capacity of humans for thinking and learning. The connection between them lies precisely in the evolution of socially responsive mechanisms like docility.

THE MYOPIA OF EVOLUTION

If we are planning an action through conscious rational calculation, and if we are smart enough, we can look ahead through some period of time—at least a short period—and conceive of the possible consequences of the action over that period. In principle, there are no fixed limits to the time horizons that govern the calculation of the consequences of action.

Such a look-ahead capability contrasts sharply with the mechanisms of biological evolution, which provide only a very myopic kind of rationality. Fitness tends to select out those organisms that secure an immediate short-run advantage. The organism, from whatever starting point it finds itself, climbs up the local hill of fitness.

Local and Global Maxima

In a very simple world, short-run advantage would convert continuously into long-run advantage. If you climb a hill in such a world, you eventually get to the world's highest point. But that result is guaranteed only in a world with a single hill. If the organism lives in a world that is full of eminences and depressions (having a topography like California's, say), it can find itself on top of all sorts of local hills with nowhere to go but down. And so any evolutionary argument in which fitness is seen as *maximized* by evolution holds only for local maxima. Unless we think the world has a very special and simple shape, we should not imagine that evolution will lead to anything properly describable as a global maximum.

In the more complex world with many hills, we see also that the particular path a hill-climbing effort follows can determine which hill the system will endeavor to climb. Which mutations happen to occur first can determine in which of many divergent directions the system will evolve. Nothing in the theory of natural selection predicts which particular hill will be climbed. Since the space of all possible variations of organisms is vastly too large to be explored exhaustively in the whole time of the earth's existence, there are many hills, probably some very high ones, that will never be climbed.

Various schemes have been proposed for accelerating evolution and diminishing the effects of myopia. Among these are schemes that preserve not just a single fittest genetic strain, but a large number of relatively fit strains, and allow them to evolve in parallel.[14] Since the "next-best" strains, at any given time, could be climbing different hills than the fittest, such a scheme would prevent immedi-

[14] See J. H. Holland, *Adaptation in Natural and Artificial Systems* (Ann Arbor, Mich., 1975).

ate advantage from trapping the process on the slopes of a small hill. However, as applied to biological evolution, a parallel scheme requires some protection of the "next-best" strains from direct competition with the momentarily fittest. To some extent, niche specialization could provide that protection.

We may reach the same conclusion in a slightly different way. The Darwinian process is a process of generating certain possibilities and then testing them and retaining the better ones. The achievement of a global maximum can be guaranteed by such a process only to the extent that all likely candidates are actually generated. As we have seen, if we consider even a single chromosome, with, say, 10,000 genes, each having two alleles, the history of the world does not allow time enough to generate more than a tiny fraction of the $10^{3,000}$ possibilities.

The possible relevance of global optimization becomes even more doubtful if the landscape that supports the hill-climbing effort is not stationary. If we have a landscape of evolving, elaborating niches—so that hills spring up everywhere, so to speak—then we can conceive of a process of evolution that doesn't lead to anything one could call an optimum, or even a stable equilibrium. Evolution in such a world continually opens up new possibilities, new combinations. Even at the inorganic level, we see that there has been such an evolution. At one time conditions were such that only a few of the elements could exist in a stable state. Through the combinatorial processes, there gradually evolved the great complexity that we see today in the biological and social worlds.

One important kind of evidence that evolution does not lead to optimization and stability was introduced by Darwin himself, although he introduced it for a very different reason.[15] He referred to the many known instances in which an alien species, introduced into a new island or continent, has run riot thanks to its superior fitness in the new environment and has eliminated native species. He took these instances to be evidence—as they are—of the power of the forces of natural selection. They are equally evidence of the nonoptimal and nonequilibrium state of the world of evolving organisms. If, for example, the North American biota had reached an optimum of fitness prior to the introduction of the English sparrow, the sparrow could not have found a niche. Its invention, as it were, would have been anticipated.

The success of introduced species, then, is strong evidence for the incompleteness of the evolutionary generator and the consequent inability of the system to reach an optimum. In a relative sense, the *fitter* survive, but there is no reason to suppose that they are the *fittest* in any absolute sense, or that we can even define what we mean by maximum fitness.

If we had lived in the Cretaceous Period, we might have imagined that the dinosaurs were highly fit, and so they were. It is widely thought that they lost their fitness when they were unable to adapt to a relatively rapid (perhaps even sudden) change in their environment. But can we be sure that they would not again be highly fit in some parts of our contemporary world? Perhaps we do not find them

[15] *Origin of Species*, 6th ed. (1872), chap. 12.

here only because they have not been reinvented, and not because they are deficient in fitness for some class of present-day niches. If this is conceivably true of dinosaurs, creatures that at one time were actually generated by the evolutionary process, it appears even more plausible as applied to some subset, large or small, of the immense domain of possible creatures that have simply never been generated.

Searching Without Final Goals

It follows that the teleology of the evolutionary process is of a rather peculiar sort. There is no goal, only a process of searching and ameliorating. Searching is the end. I suggested earlier that evolution is sometimes regarded as a preferred explanation for rationality precisely because it doesn't require a detailed explanation of process; the important thing is adaptation, however the adaptation is brought about. Evolution permits one to postulate the ends without specifying the means. Now we see that the matter is really the other way around. Evolution, at least in a complex world, specifies means (the processes of variation and selection) that do not lead to any predictable end. From ends without means, we have come full circle to means without ends.

Let me pursue a parallel idea with respect to human culture, and specifically with respect to the development of science and technology. Science and technology are not things, like automobiles and power plants, but are the knowledge and computational power that allow us to create such things, and allow us also to consider whether and to what extent we want to manufacture and use them.

Science and technology bring about a broadening and a deepening of our perspectives of time and space, for they allow us to generate alternatives more rapidly, and they allow better evaluation of these alternatives.

In a model of niche competition, and especially in a model of niche proliferation, we would expect the evolution of knowledge to be a vital component of the total evolutionary process. But the only goal one can see in this evolution is the proliferation of ideas, enriching the collection of concepts that exist in the world. And one can talk of that proliferation of knowledge as the end of the whole process, an end in itself.

Because traditional evolutionary theories focus on adaptation to a fixed environment, they speak about ends. The ends they speak about are the ends of adaptation, of maximizing fitness to the environment. But evolutionary theories that emphasize the elaboration of niches describe a system that is not evolving toward any particular end, except perhaps some kind of growth of complexity.

Human beings, at least some of us, are saddened from time to time by the notion that the world may be a closed space. Perhaps some of you were bothered, as children or adults, by the fact that Columbus had already discovered the New World, and that there wasn't another world to be discovered. One motive for space travel is that it provides the opportunity to reach new worlds that have not yet been occupied. Many people apparently yearn for a vision of a world that is not closed, in which there never comes a time when we say, "Well, now we know everything that is to be known, and we've done everything that is to be done." A world of evolving niches, a world of continually increasing complexity, is a world, whatever its other properties, in which we do not have this particular concern.

Let me try now to draw the threads together. What does an evolutionary viewpoint toward rational processes imply? First, the acceptance of evolution (and hence of its kind of rationality) does not commit us to a viewpoint of global optimization, to the idea that everything is evolving to some stationary optimal state. It commits us only to the belief that there is lots of local adaptation to the current environment, and at the same time constant movement toward a target that is itself continually moving.

Second, an evolutionary model of rationality does not commit us to a particular mechanism for the rational process. It only suggests the directions in which the process may move.

Third, the Darwinian version of evolution, postulating variation and selection, requires us to take very seriously the notion of the selfish gene. Especially in the fixed-niche model, it is hard to find room for anything except a kind of selfishness. But a closer look shows that there are in fact powerful mechanisms, the various feedback mechanisms that I described earlier, that can force selfishness to be enlightened if it is to increase fitness. When there is appropriate feedback, unenlightened selfishness can experience problems for survival as great as those experienced by pure altruism. Hence, in a Darwinian world we must expect to observe many behaviors that in ordinary speech would be described as altruistic, although the altruism may actually be rewarded through one or more of the indirect paths we have considered.

Fourth, the most powerful and prominent processes of competition in the real world may not be competition to occupy a fixed set of niches, but processes of specialization and niche elaboration. Hence we don't have to adopt a picture of the world that is all tooth and claw.

Evolutionary theory does place strong, if abstract, limitations on the class of possible worlds. It does say that a world can't continue to exist for any length of time in which there are large numbers of creatures that are less well adapted to their environments than their existing competitors are. The former creatures will simply disappear in the competition.

So evolutionary theory does make predictions, at least to the extent of telling us that some sorts of worlds are not possible worlds, hence not worlds we should plan for. In this sense, evolutionary theory is anti-utopian. But, whatever its restrictions, it does not bind us into a straitjacket of consistent maximization. Nor does it require us to accept narrow selfishness as the only human motive that can survive.

Finally, if we compare evolutionary theory with the three models of human rationality that we described in the previous chapter, we see that it resembles most closely the behavioral model. In both theories, searching a large space of possibilities and evaluating the products of that search are the central mechanisms of adaptation. Both theories are myopic. Such optimization as they achieve is only local. They are best described not as optimization processes, but as mechanisms capable of discovering new possibilities that are "improvements" over those attained earlier.

In the following chapter, we will look at the implications of these characteristics of adaptive processes for the application of rationality to human social affairs. We will ask what bounded human rationality can contribute to choice and planning in a complex world.

3. Rational Processes in Social Affairs

WHY TALK ABOUT social decision making? Isn't it enough to talk about individual decision making? Why do we need social decision making at all? Today there is abroad in the land the libertarian delusion that individuals are some sort of Leibnizian monads (little hard spheres of some kind), each with a consistent independent utility function and each interacting with its fellows only through its knowledge of market prices. Not so. We are not monads because, among many other reasons, our values, the alternatives of action that we are aware of, our understanding of what consequences may flow from our actions—all this knowledge, all these preferences—derive from our interaction with our social environment. Some of our values and knowledge were sucked in with our mother's milk; others were taken, often quite uncritically, from our social environment. Still others, perhaps, were acquired by reacting against that environment, but few indeed, surely, in complete independence of it.

What is the statistical probability, in a model of independent random variation, that in 1970 or thereabouts several million American students should regard themselves as radicals, and that ten years later a comparable majority should decide that the middle of the road is the best part to walk on? As this and innumerable other phenomena attest, beliefs and values are highly contagious from one person to another. An inventory of the beliefs of even the most self-consciously rational among us would show that most of those beliefs gain their credibility, not from direct experience and experiment, but from their acceptance by credible and "legitimate" sources in the society.

In our society, and most other modern societies, markets in which people exchange goods for money play a very important role. But markets do not operate in a social vacuum; they are part of a wider framework of social institutions. And they operate with many externalities: that is to say, many consequences of the actions taken in market economies are not fully incorporated in market prices. Typical examples are the smoke that blows from your chimney into your neighbor's eyes, or the sound pollution that wafts across your fence from his stereo. In every society, and particularly in an urban society, many of the ways our actions affect other people's lives and values cannot be easily mediated by adjusting market prices.

And just as negative externalities are not appropriately penalized by laissez-faire markets, so the production of public goods is not appropriately rewarded. Many things in society that we enjoy we do not pay for. Every morning in Pittsburgh, I receive some public goods (very valuable to me) when I walk to work. I get these goods from the fact that my neighbors keep their lawns nicely green and trimmed, and maintain lovely plantings of shrubs and flowers. When the owners of some vacant land along my daily route began, a year ago, to erect some rather ugly condominiums, my free income, my public good, was in that measure diminished. But that diminution was not reflected in the market prices of those condominiums; the new owners did not have to recompense me for my loss, any more than I have to pay for gazing at my neighbors' flowers. As a result, more ugly buildings are erected than would be if these indirect effects impinged on the decision makers, and gardens are more modest than would be optimal if the pleasure of viewers were taken into account.

Externalities, positive and negative, are woven through the whole fabric of society. They are important determinants of the rewards that individuals receive, thereby vitiating the basic libertarian argument that the state has no right to interfere with those rewards. What determines poverty or affluence? What information about a newborn child will best predict the level of comfort it will attain as an adult? First, its decade of birth, second its native land, third the status of its family. By any reasonable theory of causation, these largely explain why very many of us in twentieth-century America or Sweden are affluent, and why most people in China and India are poor. We were born at the right or wrong time and place, in families that could or could not give us a head start in the race.

Even if we accept the argument that the products attributable wholly to individual effort are inviolate, that argument places little of the world's income beyond the legitimate reach of taxation or control. If we believe, nevertheless, that the state should exercise great restraint in redistributing rewards, it must be because the prospect of redistribution may weaken people's motivation to produce, not because redistribution is ethically "unfair."

So it's all very well to talk about coming as close as we can to this state of monadism we call individualism, but at best the approximation will be very rough indeed. All our behavior takes place within an intricate environment of institutions, and has innumerable effects on other people. Market structures are no substitute for the whole web of social interactions, nor do they justify libertarian policies.

Social institutions, and particularly political institutions, have a bad press today. We describe political institutions, especially, in stereotypic fashion. We refer to them as bureaucracies, and we take it for granted that they will operate inefficiently. But there is another way of looking at institutions. As was argued in the first two chapters, we are all very limited in how fully we can calculate our actions and in how rational we can be in a complicated world. But institutions provide a stable environment for us that makes at least a modicum of rationality possible. We can reliably expect, for example, that if we walk two blocks in a certain direction, we will find a food store, and that the store will still be there tomorrow. We rely on these stabilities of our institutional environment, and many others much less superficial, to be able to make reasonable and stable calculations about the consequences of our behavior.

Thus, our institutional environment, like our natural environment, surrounds us with a reliable and perceivable pattern of events. We do not have to understand the underlying causal mechanisms that produce these events, or the events themselves in all their detail, but only their pattern as it impinges on our life, on our needs and wants. The stabilities and predictabilities of our environment, social and natural, allow us to cope with it within the limits set by our knowledge and our computational capacities.

THE LIMITS OF INSTITUTIONAL RATIONALITY

In this chapter I want to discuss institutions, but not with the aim of making simple heroes of them. On the contrary, I would like also to indicate some ways in which the limits of our individual rationality—our individual ability to calculate effective courses of action—create problems for the design and operation of our social institutions. My emphasis will be on how the limits on our ability to calculate and to behave in a reasonable fashion impose similar limits on the capabilities of our institutions.

Limits of Attention

The first problem for social behavior arising from human psychological limits is that our political institutions, particularly when they are dealing with the "big" problems, must attend to these problems in a serial, one-at-a-time (or at best a-few-at-a-time) fashion. Unfortunately, the entire range of public problems that need to be dealt with cannot be on the active agenda simultaneously. The reason is that when questions are important and controversial (and if they are important, they are usually also controversial), they have to be settled by democratic procedures that require the formation of majorities in legislative bodies or in the electorate as a whole. Consequently, the voters or the legislators must for periods of time attend simultaneously to more or less the same thing. Committees of a legislature, of course, may operate in parallel, but at various points in time the entire body must spend time reaching a consensus on the important issues.

The difficulty of focusing attention on more than a few issues at a time produces at least two phenomena, which, though they exist side by side, appear at first blush to be somewhat contradictory. The first phenomenon is the faddish quality of the behavior of political institutions. Toward the end of the 1960's, environmental problems were faddish. By faddish I mean nothing bad, simply that a large part of the available political attention was focused on these matters. During that time it was possible to obtain legislative approval for many kinds of new regulations designed to protect and improve the quality of the environment.

Then suddenly in 1973, with the first oil shock, we learned that we might not have all the energy we wanted to use, or at least might have to pay a very large price for it. We were suddenly an energy-aware society, obsessed with the energy scarcity and particularly the scarcity of petroleum. In trying to deal with this new crisis, we were (and still are) in serious danger of neglecting our concern with protecting the environment. In the context of our political institutions, it seems difficult to remember that a society may have more than one pressing problem at a time.

As another example, we became very concerned with inflation a half dozen years ago, and soon we were pointing all our economic policies toward reducing inflationary

pressures. While we were focusing our attention on inflation, we forgot that economies were also supposed to be
productive, that they were supposed to employ people in
useful work so that they could earn money to buy their
bread. In taking strong measures to deal with inflation, we
allowed unemployment to grow to levels unknown since
the Great Depression, and left a significant part of our
productive resources unutilized. What then? Unemployment began to compete with inflation for public attention,
but with a real possibility that the employment problem
may be solved by allowing inflation to gain new momen-
tum. We seem to have a very difficult time in our society
focusing attention on two problems of this kind simultaneously, even problems so closely linked that any measures we take to deal with one will almost surely affect the
other.

Some people in our society are less susceptible than the
majority of us to the fads I have just described; they suffer
from a different aberration. These are the people whose
political interests are essentially confined to a single issue,
whether it be abortion or the avoidance of abortion, gun
control or freedom to own firearms, school prayers or
freedom from religious coercion. Such people react to
whatever happens to be on the political agenda primarily
in terms of how it affects their favorite issue. Their vote on
candidates for office is determined by the candidates' posi-
tions on the single issue that obsesses them.

M. D. Cohn, J. G. March, and J. P. Olsen have developed an interesting model of this phenomenon, to which
they have given the inelegant title of "A Garbage Can

Model of Organizational Choice."[1] Their idea is that there are permanent issues, and people permanently attached to these issues, in any society or organization. When any particular matter comes up for decision, these permanent buzzing issues descend on it and take over the debate. The organization is never deciding what it purports to be deciding. The curriculum committee's formal question is whether requiring course X or course Y would be better for some group of students. What is really debated is how requiring course X or course Y would affect the number of faculty slots in departments A and B.

Both political faddishness and one-issue politics stem from the same underlying cause: people's inability to think about a lot of things at once. As a consequence, political institutions that are supposed to be dealing with a whole range of problems in the society sometimes have great difficulty in giving them balanced attention.

Happily, this difficulty is mitigated a bit by a characteristic of the world that was mentioned in the first chapter: the fact that not everything is connected closely with everything else. The examples I picked of the difficulties derived from people's limited attention span were chosen to emphasize the difficulty. Energy and environment, for example, are much more closely linked than would be most pairs of problems picked at random. Many of the things one could do to solve an energy problem might create or intensify environmental problems. Thus, for example, if you burn increased quantities of fossil fuels, the average temperature of the earth may increase because of the car-

[1] *Administrative Science Quarterly* 17: 1–25 (1972).

bon dioxide effect; and this would be perilous because, as everyone knows, the earth is exactly the right temperature—or at least human artifacts and institutions are generally adapted to the temperatures that now prevail. The same point is illustrated by the inflation-unemployment example. You can't deal satisfactorily with one member of the pair without taking account of the other.

But the network of interconnections among problems is not dense. Morever, particular problems that are repetitive, or that can be anticipated, can be handled in parallel; that is, once we have settled on policies for them and agreed on procedures to implement these policies, we can set up parallel organizations to carry out the procedures. The Fire Department can go its raucous way with only intermittent attention from the City Council, and it can operate at the same time the Police Department is arresting burglars and the Public Works Department is filling potholes. Just as in an individual human being the heartbeat goes on regularly without anyone attending to it (it's when it skips a beat that it gets attention), so the routine needs of a society can be handled in parallel. But adaptation to the novel and the unexpected does require focusing attention on them.

Even matters that are independent in other respects may become interdependent where they make demands on the same scarce resources. How is military security related to social welfare? By the fact that if you spend your dollars for one, you don't have them to spend for the other. For this reason, the governmental budgetary process often becomes the focus of the interdependence of the different needs, wants, and goals of the society.

Multiple Values

Another problem deriving from the limited rationality of individual human beings is that our political and social institutions have no easy or magic way of dealing with multiple values like those represented by the conflicting goals I have been discussing. We have no automatic formulas, no numbers to compute, that will tell us just how much emphasis we should put on improving the environment and just how much on meeting our energy needs. Likewise, we have no magic way of dealing with the problem of conflicting interests—the problem that each one of us may weigh these values in a different way.

The difficulty is epitomized in Kenneth Arrow's celebrated social welfare theorem, which demonstrates, under quite plausible assumptions regarding the conditions a social welfare function should satisfy, that no such function can exist. Among the reasonable assumptions underlying Arrow's theorem is the postulate that different people are to be allowed to weight their values in different ways—that we don't want to force all people to have the same set of values. If we accept assumptions like these, we discover that we really don't know how to compare values between people; it's a matter of apples and oranges. Thus, under some plausible assumptions about the diversity we want to permit in human choice, we are unable to define a social welfare function that would solve the problem of conflict of interest.

Uncertainty

A third difficulty that social organizations inherit from the cognitive limitations of their members is difficulty in

84

dealing with problems of uncertainty. None of us like wars. In fact, in this day and age we think of wars as particularly unpleasant, more unpleasant than they've ever been in human history. But at the same time we have no clear idea whether various actions we might take will make war more probable or less probable. Will taking a hard line with the USSR (or a soft line) increase or decrease the probability of war? Many of us have opinions on this issue; few of us attach high certainty to our opinions. Over our society as a whole, such certainties as there are about this and similar matters are conflicting certainties; so we have great difficulties in agreeing on a course of action.

In the face of even moderate uncertainty, it seems almost hopeless to strive for "optimal" courses of action. When conflicts in values exist, as they almost always do, it is not even clear how "optimal" is to be defined. But all is not lost. Reconciling alternative points of view and different weightings of values becomes somewhat easier if we adopt a *satisficing* point of view: if we look for *good enough* solutions rather than insisting that only the best solutions will do. It may be possible—and it often is possible—to find courses of action that almost everyone in a society will tolerate, and that many people will even like, provided we aren't perfectionists who demand an optimum.

Many of the problems created by uncertainty are captured by the Prisoner's Dilemma game. Two persons have been arrested by the police and charged with a serious crime. Without confessions the evidence is adequate only to convict them on lesser charges, in which event both will receive only moderate punishment. The police inform each prisoner that if he confesses he will receive a still milder punishment, but they will "throw the book" at his partner; whereas if they both confess, each will be punished fairly severely but much less so than Prisoner A would be if only Prisoner B confessed. What is the rational course of action for the two prisoners?

Prisoner A observes that if B confesses, he (A) will be punished much less severely if he also confesses. But if B does not confess, he (A) will also lighten his own punishment (at B's expense) by confessing. Thus, under either circumstance, it is rational for A to confess. By the same reasoning, it is rational for B to confess. But if both confess, they are much worse off than if neither had confessed.

The analogy of the Prisoner's Dilemma to a nuclear standoff is frighteningly close. How do we make it appear rational to the participants to act with restraint instead of making a first strike? But the dilemma does not appear only in this extreme form; it arises in many bilateral situations in which there is a conflict of interest—in labor negotiations, for example, where it is almost always better for both sides to avert a strike than to precipitate one. Yet it may be hard to stabilize the system in the no-strike state.

Even the assumption that the game is to be played not just once, but repeatedly, does not help matters much. It remains "advantageous"—at least by many definitions of rationality—to take aggressive action against the opponent before he can take aggressive action against you. However, empirical studies of humans playing repeated Prisoner's Dilemma games, and computer runs of sequences of simulated games between players using different strategies, show a less grim picture.[2] Players fre-

[2] See A. Rapoport and A. M. Chammah, *Prisoner's Dilemma* (Ann Arbor, Mich., 1965); R. Axelrod, "Effective Choice in the Prisoner's Dilemma," *Journal of Conflict Resolution* 24: 13–25, 379–403 (1980).

quently adopt relatively benign strategies, and are usually reasonably well rewarded for doing so. In contests between different computer strategies, the strategy of tit-for-tat does particularly well. This strategy calls for taking the benign action until the opponent aggresses; then switching for one round to the aggressive action; and then, as soon as the opponent retreats to the benign action, doing likewise.

Roy Radner[3] has shown formally that if one's goal is not to optimize but simply to reach a satisfactory level of return, the tit-for-tat strategy can be rational. His result provides one possible explanation for the frequent human propensity to settle on this strategy. Nevertheless, the basic Prisoner's Dilemma paradigm shows us how brittle are the mechanisms of rationality in the face of uncertainty, and especially in the face of uncertainty about the actions of another party where there is partial conflict of interest.

STRENGTHENING INSTITUTIONAL RATIONALITY

The institutional limitations just discussed are rather basic, being rooted in the limits of individual rationality. Nevertheless some institutional arrangements are better suited than others to responding rationally to problems of social choice. Organizations may be created to deal with the interrelatedness of decisions. Market structures may reduce the actors' needs for comprehensive information. Adversary proceedings may provide some protection against neglecting or ignoring relevant facts and values. There are a number of familiar ways in which these and

---

[3] Personal communication.

other mechanisms can be used to strengthen the role of reason in social choice. I should like to comment briefly on some of them.

Organizations and Markets

First, the routine and repetitive requirements of a society are handled in parallel by creating specialized groups and organizations, each of which deals with one set of issues while the others are dealing with the remainder. If it were not so obvious, we might label this the "fundamental theorem of organization theory."

Second, over a wide range of matters, we can use markets and pricing to limit the amount of information each person must have about the decisions he is going to make. When I go to the local supermarket, I can decide what to buy and what I am going to eat without knowing very much about how Wheaties and oatmeal are made, or what the manufacturer's problems are. I need only know the price at which he is offering these commodities to me. For this reason, markets and prices have proved to be extremely powerful mechanisms in modern societies for helping each of us to make decisions without having to learn a whole lot of detail about other people who may be involved. All the relevant information is summed up in the price we have to pay in order to make the transaction.

This is a very different argument for markets than the optimization argument one finds in some economics books. Under very stringent assumptions, involving perfect competition as well as perfect rationality, markets can be shown to lead to a Pareto optimum—that is, an equilibrium such that not everyone's welfare can be increased simultaneously; for some to gain further, others must lose.

The Pareto optimum is not unique; there may be many such optima, different subsets of participants being favored by different solutions. However, optima are not my concern here. I am presenting the more basic and general argument, made many years ago by Hayek, that even without assumptions of perfect competition and perfect rationality markets provide a way of restricting how much we need to know about everyone else's business in order to do our own. The market mechanism may provide a way to reach tolerable arrangements in a society even if optimality is beyond reach.

Thus the market can be viewed as one of the mechanisms that enable human beings having limited information and computational capacity to operate more or less intelligently. Today we see the interesting spectacle of the socialist nations dealing with some of their problems of planning and management by a broader introduction of pricing and market mechanisms. They are trying to dissociate the issue of markets from the issue of public versus private ownership in order to use prices as a major tool for allocating resources. To be sure, when we talk about such uses of the price mechanism, we must keep in mind that the externalities discussed earlier are rarely absent. Markets can only be used in conjunction with other methods of social control and decision making; they do not provide an independent mechanism for social choice.

We could be more ingenious than we are today in using price mechanisms effectively where externalities are present. Economists have made many suggestions along these lines—for example, setting penalties for emitting smoke that would be commensurate at the margin with the damage and nuisance of the smoke. Still, even if we extended such procedures to their practical limits, there would remain many market externalities—either negative externalities or public goods. Some, for example those with important consequences for health or public safety, would be subject, as today, to direct limitations or regulations.

Adversary Proceedings

Adversary proceedings are another way of strengthening rationality. I suppose we can call many legislative processes, especially legislative hearings and debates, adversary proceedings. But we use the adversary process most extensively in our judicial system, where the criterion for rationality is a most interesting one. The basic criterion of justice, which surely aims at satisficing rather than optimizing, is that specified procedures be followed. The underlying assumption is that if these procedures are followed, then, in some long-run sense, the decisions reached will be tolerable, or even desirable. Hence in legal institutions we tend to evaluate outcomes not so much directly as in terms of procedural fairness.

Adversary proceedings are like markets in reducing the information that participants must have in order to behave rationally. Thus they provide a highly useful mechanism for systems in which information is distributed widely and in which different system components have different goals. Each participant in an adversary proceeding is supposed to understand thoroughly his own interests and the factual considerations relating to them. He need not understand the interests or situations of the other participants. Each pleads his own cause, and in doing so, contributes to the general pool of knowledge and understanding.

In order for adversary proceedings to work well, the

right to become a party to any process must be defined broadly enough so that all who will be significantly affected by the decision have an opportunity to contribute their evidence and voice their preferences. In our own society the notion of interdependence has been increasingly recognized; the courts have steadily broadened the rules determining who may be heard in any particular case, even one that begins as a dispute between two specific parties. In this way, the courts take account of externalities analogous to those that arise in the workings of a market system.

Technical Tools for Decision

Finally, there has been an important development in the last thirty years in the technical means available for making decisions about situations with many variables and many interconnections among them. These new tools are usually assigned to the disciplines of operations research and management science—and today to artificial intelligence as well. It is a special characteristic of these tools that they allow us to formulate, model, and solve problems with thousands of variables and thousands of constraints on the variables, and to take account of the interactions of all these variables and constraints in arriving at a solution.

One serious limitation on the applicability of operations research and management science techniques is that they require problems to be quantified in such a way that known mathematical techniques become applicable to them. For example, to employ linear programming for solving a problem, the problem first has to be translated (or folded, or beaten) into a form that expresses it in terms of linear equations, linear constraints, and a linear payoff function. If the world doesn't have these properties, or can't be approximated adequately in this way, linear programming won't work. Artificial intelligence techniques, by contrast, do not usually require problems to be mathematized, but can deal with qualitative considerations or situations that are wholly qualitative. Consequently, they are substantially extending the range of problems in which the modern computer can increase the power of human analysis.

Despite various limitations, these new methods have allowed us to look at some of the difficult problems in our world with a concern for side effects and interactions that simply could not have been encompassed before these tools were introduced shortly after World War II. If we do find solutions (as I think we will) for the difficult problems of environment and energy—solutions, that is, that handle both sets of problems simultaneously—it will be because we are able to model the main interactions among the many facets of these problems, and hence to think clearly about tradeoffs.

The new analytic tools mark at least one modest step of progress, and provide at least one reason for optimism about our capacity to deal with the increasingly complicated problems which the world is presenting to us.

THE PUBLIC INFORMATION BASE

The other major concern in getting our institutions to make reasonable decisions on big policy questions is the adequacy of our knowledge and information. In the first chapter, I argued that the effectiveness of reason as a tool for making decisions depends critically on the facts that it takes as its inputs—the data, the knowledge, and the theories that it uses as its givens. Unless those inputs are valid, nothing is gained by manipulating them. If you put bad data or incorrect knowledge into a human thought process, you will get wrong conclusions out the far end.

The Mass Media

How adequate is the knowledge base for public policy decisions? All of us, I think, are prepared to point out the vagaries of the mass media, and to describe what we don't like about the particular media that displease us most. There seems to be general agreement that there are serious difficulties with the media as major sources of the facts and knowledge we use in the public decision-making process.

Perhaps the most fundamental difficulty is that the media rarely look beyond the news and the fads of the present moment. They emphasize the newsworthy, the sensational, the novel. TV is perhaps even a worse offender than the older media on this dimension because it can create not only a local trend, but a national or international focus of attention. But even the older media tend to traffic in news rather than in understanding. For example, a person seeking a factually grounded view of American foreign policy toward China is much better advised to read one or two good books than to read everything he can find about China in the *New York Times* over the next year. The newspaper will give him a miscellany of transient facts. The books will provide a solid, and only slowly changing, framework that will make current events coherent and understandable.

What one really needs to know in order to have an

informed view on such a topic is some understanding of Chinese institutions and Chinese history—precisely the kinds of information that are hard to come by in the periodical media. The media are busy telling what the action is today, this week. But what's happening today in China is just the product of underlying characteristics and trends in Chinese society, and can't begin to be interpreted correctly by persons who haven't read the right books.

The transient character of most of the information obtainable from the media would be of little consequence if attention were not a terribly scarce resource. The time spent reading the newspaper or watching TV is then no longer available for acquiring conceptual frameworks and background information—the very information that would make the reports of more transitory events intelligible. I suppose a society that became highly sensitive to the scarcity of attention might modify its reading habits to allocate attention more efficiently. Although in our own society complaints about the flood of information are common enough, there is little evidence of people deliberately designing strategies to protect themselves from the transient and the evanescent. It seems a novel idea to many people that news need not be ingested simply "because it is there."

Experts

But even if we banished information of transitory value from our diets, how would we choose our books? After the responsible citizen reads the books on China, he has to read one on Afghanistan, and there is no end of books. We all feel the overwhelming difficulty of being appropriately informed. But we do have ways of dealing with that difficulty, in matters of public policy as in matters of medicine or plumbing: we turn to experts. When we can't establish the relevant facts, we look for an expert who knows them and we listen to what he has to say. Sometimes we even take his advice without asking to have it fully explained.

How do we find experts who are really expert? How do we accredit and legitimate the experts? Although we don't always do it very well, our society and other developed societies have been learning how to do it better. For example, the United States Congress has been turning more and more for information and advice to the National Academy of Sciences and its affiliated organizations, the National Academy of Engineering, the Institute of Medicine, and the National Research Council. This group of institutions is in a position to identify and draw on most of the scientific, medical, and engineering expertise in our country on any topic relevant to current public policy deliberations.

But how are we sure that these (or any others) are the right experts? And how do we keep the experts honest—how do we make sure their own interests do not color the advice they give? At one level, the problem of interest-colored advice is solved easily, at another level not easily at all. It is easy to require that experts disclose financial ties or professional responsibilities that might lead to a conflict of interest in providing information and advice. In calling on experts in our society today, as when the government seeks advice through the organizations named above, such a requirement of disclosure is routine.

But there is a more subtle question of conflict of interest

that derives directly from human bounded rationality. The fact is, if we become involved in a particular activity and devote an important part of our lives to that activity, we will surely assign it a greater importance and value than we would have prior to our involvement with it. If a man makes a living designing nuclear power plants, it is a good bet that he would be unlikely to sign a petition against building a nuclear plant in your town. You probably would not even bother to ask, but would look elsewhere for a signer.

It's very hard for us, sometimes, not to draw from such facts a conclusion that human beings are rather dishonest creatures. Whose food they eat, his songs they sing. Yet most of the bias that arises from human occupations and preoccupations cannot be described correctly as rooted in dishonesty—which perhaps makes it more insidious than if it were.

Human beings don't see the whole world; they see the little part of it they live in, and they are capable of making up all sorts of rationalizations about that part of the world, mostly in the direction of aggrandizing its importance. Let me pursue the nuclear power example a little further, for it provides many excellent illustrations of the phenomenon. More than ten years ago, when two whistle blowers at Livermore Laboratory produced some statistics allegedly showing that health dangers from radiation in the vicinity of nuclear plants were substantially greater than had been thought, the first reaction of people associated with nuclear power was to close ranks. With few exceptions, they did not say, "Let's look into this more closely.

Let's appoint an impeccable blue-ribbon commission to find the facts." On the contrary, the almost universal reaction was, "Why are those irresponsible fellows shooting off their mouths?"

I was relatively close to these events as a member of the President's Science Advisory Committee at that time, and recall being naïvely surprised at the insensitivity of the "insiders" to the depth of public concern. Many of the "insiders" were my friends or acquaintances, persons of high integrity, whom I did not suspect of venality in any form. What blinded them to the need for an impartial look at the facts was the "knowledge" they had acquired, through years of association with the development of nuclear energy; the conviction that this technology was a boon to mankind, opening up new kinds of productivity, relieving us of our dependence on exhaustible fossil fuels, and surely not creating any unusual dangers to health that had not already been foreseen and dealt with. The depth of their commitment prevented them from considering objectively whether the evidence was on their side.

When an issue becomes highly controversial—when it is surrounded by uncertainties and conflicting values—then expertness is very hard to come by, and it is no longer easy to legitimate the experts. In these circumstances, we find that there are experts for the affirmative and experts for the negative. We cannot settle such issues by turning them over to particular groups of experts. At best, we may convert the controversy into an adversary proceeding in which we, the laymen, listen to the experts but have to judge between them.

Knowledge of Political Institutions

Among the deficiencies in our knowledge that interfere with our effectiveness as participants in the political process are inadequacies in our understanding of political institutions themselves. There are a lot of things only partly understood about human beings that we would really need to know to be effective and responsible participants in the political process.

For example, the correct design of political institutions depends on a sound appreciation of the perfectibility of man. Certain political and economic arrangements will work only if all or most human beings placed under those arrangements will behave altruistically, or at least conformably with social needs. The New Society must produce a New Man. In our lifetime at least two major social revolutions, the Russian and the Chinese, have been predicated on the assumption that by changing institutions one can change human behavior. Most of us have concluded that neither revolution produced the desired changes in behavior. Yet the question persists: is there some kind of change in social institutions that will, in fact, change human beings in fundamental ways—make them, say, more altruistic or obedient to law? Debates on the treatment of criminals usually hinge on just this question.

The evolutionary arguments of Chapter 2 suggest that behavior can indeed be changed by institutions, at least to the extent of increasing or decreasing weak altruism. The possibility of producing permanent deep changes—in docility, say—is more problematic. Today there is little empirical foundation for clear answers to these questions unless we take the negative evidence from the revolutions as decisive.

With respect to other important issues, however, there does exist scientific knowledge that could help us design and choose more effective political institutions and procedures, knowledge that political scientists have been accumulating and testing for some time. In our society, we have an unfortunate habit of labeling our political institutions in two different ways. On the days when we are happy with them, we call them democracy; on the days when we are unhappy with them, we call them politics. We don't choose to recognize that "politics," used in that pejorative way, is simply a label for some of the characteristics of our democratic political institutions that we happen not to fancy. Neither "politics" nor "democracy" wholly describes those institutions, and we solve no problems by labeling their wanted and unwanted aspects in this particular way.

Some years ago I accepted the chairmanship of a committee charged with reviewing Pennsylvania's controversial milk price control law. Some of the other members of the committee were dairy farmers, and others were milk dealers or officials of the milk truck drivers' union. There were also two members who were supposed to represent consumers, and two "public members" with no direct interest in the milk industry. Around the committee table at meetings hardly an hour ever passed without one of my committee members pounding the table and inveighing against "politicians." At one time or another virtually all the members indulged in this behavior, and they were completely unselfconscious about it. It never occurred to them that as members of that committee (much more as lobbyists, which many of them were also) they were politicians. For them, "politician" was simply a cussword, a term they couldn't imagine applying to themselves.

This naïveté about politics and politicians pervades our society. It is very damaging to our political institutions. We would do well to view these institutions with greater sophistication; we would do well to recognize that they have warts. We can try to remove the warts, but we must recognize that certain kinds of political phenomena—the attempt to influence legislation or the administration of laws, the advocacy of special interest—are essential to the operation of political institutions in a society where there is, in fact, great diversity of interest, and where most people are expected to pay some attention to their own private interests. The activities we call "political" are simply another manifestation of the propensity of human beings to identify with personal goals and to attempt to realize these goals in a lawful manner.

Related to our fallacious beliefs about politics and democracy are some notions we hold about the basis of voting. There is a widespread belief in our society (or at least behavior consistent with such a belief) that after watching and listening to a candidate on television, one can make predictions about how he will act if elected to office. On the contrary, there is a large body of evidence from social-psychological experiments that human beings watching other human beings (particularly watching them emit words that are intended to be influential) are exceedingly poor predictors of what these words mean and what they imply in terms of behavior. There is good evidence, for example, that if a viewer is already favorably disposed toward a candidate, he will interpret the candidate's statements, whatever they may be, as agreeing with his own position on the issue; whereas if the viewer is disposed unfavorably toward the candidate, he will interpret the same statements as disagreeing with his position.

So here we all are, glued to our television sets, listening to campaign speeches and supposing that somehow or other we are obtaining information relevant to our decision how to vote. We even have a slogan to justify our conduct: "Vote for the man, not for the party." Suppose that we are interested in predicting what decisions a successful candidate will make during his term of office, and that in particular we wish these decisions to be as nearly in accord with our own values as possible. Is what we can learn from television or other media about the candidate's personal qualities a better or worse predictor of his subsequent behavior than his party affiliation? All the evidence I know of, and there is a good deal of it, indicates that party affiliation is by far the more reliable predictor.

The growing pride of voters in being "independent" of party loyalties has greatly weakened political parties in the United States. Not only has it increased the vulnerability of the political system to demagoguery, but it has significantly increased the difficulty of formulating and enacting public policies, and in particular of forming majorities that lie close to the mainstream of voters' preferences. For nearly two centuries, political parties have served as reasonably efficient mechanisms in the complex process of compromise and bargaining by which majorities are formed and public policy formulated. They are so no longer. The illusion of monadism that underlies the conception of the "independent voter," in destroying the behavioral predictability sustained by party organization, has lowered the level of civic rationality.

I wish I had a list of impeccable prescriptions for responsible citizen behavior in a democracy. Students who have had the standard university introductory courses in political science and economics appear to behave with no greater sophistication in the political arena than voters who have not taken such courses. That may be a comment on the courses, or on the incorrigibility of students. Whichever way it is interpreted, it is clear that we haven't found effective means for civic education. We haven't discovered a way to use the limited time and attention people are willing to devote to their civic education to produce a reasonable level of sophistication about how our political institutions work. We don't know how voters can draw effectively on the information that is available to them about issues and candidates—or how they should go about selecting experts whom they will trust.

Ignorance about the political process has bred cynicism, of which the pejorative use of "politics" is just one symptom. The pedestal on which "democracy" is placed only sharpens the contrast between ideal and reality. Probably the best antidotes for this cynicism are education in a realistic picture of democratic political institutions, and normative discussion of realizable goals for such institutions. But I see little sign of either in the media or in educational institutions.

Is Knowledge the Answer?

Do we have available to us (if we get access to it and would use it) the knowledge we need in order to make reasonably sensible decisions about the major issues of public policy? The answer varies, case by case. Let me propose a triad of examples that more or less span the continuum.

First, there are the very crucial, first-priority problems of war and peace. Here we have reason for pessimism, for it is not clear what kinds of information or knowledge we could gather or what kinds of scientific research we could undertake that would make it easier than it now is to penetrate the confusions and complexities of policies for maintaining peace. It is particularly difficult if we have several goals, as most of us have. We want to preserve peace; we also want to preserve essential characteristics of our institutions and of our freedoms. I find it difficult to imagine what sorts of improvements in our factual knowledge would make these problems less perplexing.

The main source of difficulty is that questions of war and peace involve not only uncertainty about our own behavior under a variety of circumstances that are hard to imagine in advance, but also uncertainty about the behaviors of other nations and the kind of outguessing game in which we are engaged. I don't know how this could be approached in a scientific way with our present scientific knowledge.

But when we turn to my second example, the problem of energy and environment, we find a whole gamut of research and development procedures that can not only help us better understand the known technological alternatives and their consequences, but also widen the range of alternatives to be considered. We know a great deal better, for example, than we did fifteen years ago, the effects on atmosphere and climate of increasing our production of carbon dioxide, or the effects of acid rain on plant growth and lake populations. And we know a great deal better how to correct these problems.

My third example, economic policy, lies somewhere in the middle of my scale of optimism. The reason is that the operation of the economy depends critically on human expectations about the future and human reactions to those expectations, and this is an exceedingly difficult domain to study.

It is fashionable today to say that if there are five different economists in a room, there are five different opinions about how the economy operates and how to improve its operation. In a way, that is true. By proper selection of the experts (requiring or not, as you please, that all hold doctorates in economics), you can get any advice you want about national economic policies. Yet the disagreement among economists is mostly limited to a small number of critical issues and focuses mainly on the question of how people form expectations about the future. A supply-sider will tell you that if you make investment profitable, either by making money cheap or by reducing taxes or in some other way, investment will increase substantially. A rational-expectationist will tell you that people cannot be fooled about the future; their expectations represent realistic estimates of the location of the equilibrium toward which the economic system is moving. A Keynesian makes still different assumptions about expectations.

Which is correct? Unfortunately we don't know. We simply don't have the facts about how human beings form their expectations and act on them that we would need in order to test the hypotheses of the supply-sider or the rational-expectationist—or the budget-balancer, or the monetarist, or the Keynesian. This is the principal area of disagreement today among different schools of economic thought. It's not a very large area, but it occupies an uncomfortably strategic location in the structure of economic theory and its application to public policy.

As these three examples illustrate, the vigorous pursuit of research and development in the natural and social sciences can give us important help in those areas of decision where knowledge is a prime limiting factor. But scientific knowledge is not the Philosopher's Stone that is going to solve all these problems.

CONCLUSION

I have been proposing that human reason is less a tool for modeling and predicting the general equilibrium of the whole world system, or creating a massive general model that considers all variables at all times, than it is a tool for exploring specific partial needs and problems. I see relatively little profit from the Olympian view implied by the SEU model of rationality. The evolutionary argument I developed in the second chapter against the viability of pure altruism suggests that in our formation of public policy and in our own private decision making it is probably reasonable to assume, as a first approximation, that people will act from self-interest. Hence a major task of any society is to create a social environment in which self-interest has reason to be enlightened. If we want an invisible hand to bring everything into some kind of social consonance, we should be sure, first, that our social institutions are framed to bring out our better selves, and second, that they do not require major sacrifices of self-interest by many people much of the time.

Reason, taken by itself, is instrumental. It can't select our final goals, nor can it mediate for us in pure conflicts over what final goal to pursue—we have to settle these issues in some other way. All reason can do is help us reach agreed-on goals more efficiently. But in this respect, at least, we are getting better. To some modest extent, the powers of human reason have themselves evolved, especially our ability to deal with simultaneous relations, and these new advances in our tools of reasoning can be said to represent a qualitative change in human thought. Just as the ability to put our thoughts on paper enabled us, with the invention of writing, to tackle problems of new complexity, so we have advanced and continue to advance in our ability to predict the consequences of our actions and to design new alternatives. These advances still leave us far short of being able to handle all of the world's complexities. But the world—fortunately, even the contemporary world—is mostly empty, most things being only weakly related to other things, and it is only with such a world that human reason needs to cope.

There is no danger of reaching a steady state in our society, or any other society, in which all problems have been solved. Such a state would in any event be rather dull. It would be quite enough to keep open for our descendants as wide a range of alternatives as our ancestors left for us, to solve enough of the problems that come along so that our children and our children's children will not find themselves boxed in any more narrowly than we were. That seems to me a more realizable goal for social policy than Utopia Now (or even Utopia Tomorrow). It is more reasonable than supposing that those things we call human problems have associated with them some other things called solutions, and that once we have discovered the solutions the problems will go away.

In accomplishing the more limited goal, will an appeal to enlightened self-interest suffice? That depends on what constraints we put on the enlightenment. Success depends on our ability to broaden human horizons so that people will take into account, in deciding what is to their interest, a wider range of consequences. It depends on whether all of us come to recognize that our fate is bound up with the fate of the whole world, that there is no enlightened or even viable self-interest that does not look to our living in a harmonious way with our total environment.

Index

Index

Adaptive mechanism, 55
Administrative Behavior, 5, 13
Adversary proceedings, 90–91
Affluence, 77
Age of Reason, 3
Agricultural society, 43
Alternatives for choice, 12, 13
Altruism, 4, 57–66, 72–73;
  weak, 58, 98
Altruistic gene, 59, 60
Archimedes, 5
Aristotle, 33
Arrow, K., vii, 84
Artificial intelligence, 22, 91–
  92
Artificial systems, 5
Attention, 21, 29–30, 79–83. *See
  also under* Emotion
Axelrod, R., 61n, 86n
Axioms, 5
Ayer, A. J., 7n

Behavioral model of rationality,
  3–5, 17–23, 28f, 30, 34; compared with natural selection,
  39–40, 73
Bounded rationality, 4, 19–23,

74; emotions in, 21; and conflict of interest, 95–96
Brain, 24; hemispheres of, 24f,
  28; search processes in, 26, 28f
Bureaucracies, 78

Campbell, D. T., viii, 40, 65n
Carson, Rachel, 30
Chammah, A. M., 86n
Chekov, Anton, 32
Chess, 25, 26, 28
Child prodigies, 28
Choosing actions, 7. *See also* De-
  cision making
Chromosomes, 47, 48, 68
Cognition: hot and cold, 29–32
Cognitive psychology, 22
Cohn, M. D., 81
Cold reasoning, 10, 30–31
Columbus and the New World,
  71
Commonsense reasoning, 22
Computational capacities, 22. *See
  also* Bounded rationality
Conflict of interest, 95–96
Creativity, 24, 27
Cretaceous Period, 69

III

INDEX

Holt, C. C., 14, 15n
Homer, 33
Hot reasoning, 10, 30, 32
Humanities, 33, 34
Hutchinson, G. E., 45n

Identification, 9–10, 95–97
Incompleteness of logic, 7
Individualism, 78
Induction: principles of, 6
Industrial society, 43
Inference rules, 5, 6
Inflation, 80–83
Instinct, 38
Institutional environment, 78
Institutional rationality: limits of, 79–87; strengthening, 87–92; and public information, 92–102; and knowledge, 102–5
Institutions, *see* Political institutions; Social institutions
Interrelated values, 11
Intuition, 24–34, 35; and emotion, 29–30
Intuitive rationality, 23–29

Joint probability distribution, 13, 14
Judgment, 24, 26; acquiring of, 27

Kahnemann, D., 17n
Kinship models, 58–59
Knowledge in social decision making, 92–105
Koestler, Arthur, 32

Laissez faire, 76
Lamarckian evolution, 49, 56
Leibnizian monads, 75
Lewontin, R. C., viii
Libertarianism, 75–78
Limits of reason, 5–7. *See also* Bounded rationality
Livermore Laboratory, 96
Lucretius, 33
Lumsden, C. J., 54n, 55

Malthus, Thomas, 53
Management science, 91
March, J. G., vii, 81
Markets, 75–78, 87–90
Mass media, 93–94
Maxima: local and global, 66, 68
Maximizing expected utility, 13. *See also* Subjective expected utility
Mayr, E., 45n
Mechanisms, 72, 87–89, 101
Mein Kampf, 8–10, 30
Microenvironment, 46
Modigliani, F., 14, 15n
Monadism, 40, 48, 59, 78, 101
Mozart, 28
Mutation, 40, 48, 67
Muth, J. R., 14, 15n
Myopia of evolution, *see under* Evolution

National Academy of Sciences, 95
Natural selection, 45, 49–50, 64–69. *See also* Fitness
Nearly empty world, 20
Nelson, Richard, 41
New Man, 98